compiled
by
THE VILLAGERS, INC.
of Miami, Florida
1987

A COOKBOOK WITH LOVING

BISCAYNE BIGHTS AND BREEZES

MEMORIES OF MIAMI

FIRST EDITION

Second Printing 3,400 Copies

Additional copies may be
obtained by writing:

BISCAYNE BIGHTS AND
BREEZES
The Villagers, Inc.
P. O. Box 141843
Coral Gables, Florida 33114

or by using the order forms
provided in the back of the book.

Library of Congress Catalog
Card Number 86-51524
ISBN 0-9617793-0-6

All proceeds from the sale of
this book will be used to
further community interest and
education in the restoration and
preservation of historic sites in
South Florida.

Printed in the United States of America
Pinnacle Group
Miami, Florida

THE VILLAGERS, INC.

The Villagers, Inc. was founded in 1966 "to further community interest in the preservation, appreciation and restoration of historical landmarks." By raising both public awareness and funds, it has contributed to the support of the following projects:

The Douglas Entrance

The Biltmore Hotel

The Casa Loma Country Club of the Biltmore Hotel

Villa Vizcaya

The Zoological Society of South Florida

Fairchild Tropical Gardens

The Historical Association of South Florida

Dade Heritage Trust

Old School House of Coconut Grove

Anderson's Corner

The Coral Gables House

"El Jardin," Carrollton School

"The Alamo," Jackson Memorial Hospital

The Flagler Workers' Cottage

Old Larkins Schoolhouse

Metropolitan Museum and Art Center

Tennessee Williams' House, Key West

Commodore Munroe's "The Barnacle"

The Brown House

The Judith Seymour Memorial Scholarship

The Charles Deering Estate

BISCAYNE BIGHTS AND BREEZES

President:

Alicia Callander, 1985-87

Editors:

Cookie Johnson

Nancy Pierce

Editorial Staff:

Allison Duncan

Louise Petrine

Alice White

Production Staff:

Susie Amerkan

Mary Bergman

Ann Brannon

Mari Brauzer

Nancy Caldwell

Tuschka Chapman

Elisabeth Cozad

Jane Dewey

Carol George

Doris Hartog

Lucy Hurst

Joan LaRoche

Aida Lazzarin

Mary Ann Martinsen

Leslie Olle

Patricia Ormond

Suzan Ponzoli

Susan Randall

Nancy Roche

Nora Robbins

Sheila Schmidt

Kay Schaffer

Geneva Waldin

Development Staff:

Mary Ann Polizzi, Chairman

Vicki Belcher

Nancy Bennett

Joan Bounds

Evelyn Chesney

Nina Derks

Kathy Gelb

Martha Halbert

Sheri LaForge

Joyce Pippo

Chris Shoffner

Dorothy Tuttle

RECIPE CONTRIBUTORS

Maxine Alspach

Susie Amerkan

Victoria Belcher

Kathy Miller Bondhus

Ann Brannon

Mari Brauzer

Alicia Callander

Tuschka Chapman

Lilly Chen

Evelyn Chesney

Sally Day

Katherine De Loach

Nina Derks

Linda Dietz

Marie Fredlund

Kathryn Gelb

Carol George

F. Kay Gerlach

Pat Godard

Martha Halbert

Doris Hartog

Nell Jennings

Cookie Johnson

Charles Kimbrell

Sevda Kursunoglu

Sheridan La Forge

Joan La Roche

Nanci Lanza

Elizabeth Le Fevre

Pat Molinari

Arlene Metz Moretz

Elizabeth Munroe

Ann Murray

Ann Palmer

Barbara Pawley

Margie Peacock

Dr. Thelma Peters

Irene Peterson

Louise Petrine

Barbara Pitcher

Mary Ann Polizzi

Polly Ramos

Nora Robbins

Irwin Sawitz

Olivia Matthews Shelley

Mary Lou Sims

Janet Stoker

Kay Sweeney

Kathy Smith Tessler

Marlies Tindall

Dorothy Tuttle

William Tuttle

Judith Tobin

Jean Van Hemert

Pam Walker

Dorinda Wenck

Alice White

Robin White

A C K N O W L E D G E M E N T S

The Villagers, Inc. wish to thank all those who worked tirelessly to make this book a reality, especially Miami's long-time residents whose memories add a "bight of history:" Dawn Hugh of the Historical Museum of Southern Florida; Ellen Uguccioni of the Historic Preservation Division of Coral Gables for photo research; Arva Moore Parks; Frank S. FitzGerald-Bush; Ivan Rodriquez of the Historic Preservation Division of Metro-Dade; Sam Boldrick and Thomas Milledge of the Florida Collection of the Miami-Dade Public Library; Kari Johnson, our computer consultant; recipe donors and testers; our editors, volunteers, and especially those who have assisted us financially.

Patrons

Anthony Abraham

Burdines

Cordis Corporation

The Dade Foundation

Mr. and Mrs. Robin White

Donors

Coral Gables Laundry and Dry Cleaning

Dr. W. W. Dolan

Mrs. Stanley Glasgow

The Stadler Companies

Walker, Ellis, Gragg & Deaktor

The photographs used are courtesy
of The Historical Association of Southern
Florida, Romer Collection at the
Miami-Dade Public Library,
Doris Littlefield of Vizcaya Museum and
Gardens, Metro-Dade Communications
and the Monroe County Tourist
Development Council.

Front Cover: The restored Casino at Vizcaya, a Villager Project

D E D I C A T I O N

Dedicated

to the memory of

Dorinda Brelsford Wenck

FOREWORD: DINING MIAMI STYLE

From the beginning of time, humans have eaten together. Archaeologists have found ancient campfires where the earliest Miamians prepared meals that included enduring South Florida favorites such as fish, oysters, turtle, clams and conch. Today, more than 10,000 years later, we still enjoy sitting down to dinner with family and friends.

A thoughtfully prepared meal, however, often does more than simply fill the stomach and lift the spirit. Culinary diplomacy has had its special place in history. Pedro Menendez de Aviles, the Spaniard who successfully settled Florida in 1565, understood the value of conviviality. After sharing a banquet with Calusa Chief Carlos, Menendez so impressed Carlos with Spanish food, silverware and hospitality that Carlos insisted he marry his sister (even though Menendez already had a wife!). But being Carlos' brother-in-law was an opportunity Menendez couldn't resist.

The 19th Century South Florida pioneers were also well known for their hospitality. Because there was no public lodging until the 1880's, it was customary for the handful of settlers to welcome all visitors to their home and hearth. After the Indian Wars ended in the late 1850's, the Seminole Indians were also welcome and they in turn brought venison and pumpkin to the table.

In Coconut Grove, South Florida's first real community, Bahamians, familiar with tropical living, taught Northerners how to eat "like a native." The Bahamians introduced such delicacies as conch fritters and conch chowder and probably invented the closest thing we have to a native food – Key lime pie.

In 1896, cold weather and the railroad brought in the Georgians and other Southern families, along with their grits and ham and biscuits and collard greens. For the next twenty years the majority of Miamians talked and ate Southern. The Boom of the 1920's contributed a lot of "Yankees," many of whom were Jewish. Before long, New York style delicatessens opened in Miami and Miami Beach and kosher pickles, bagels and cream cheese became an essential part of the Miami larder.

When the Cubans came in the 1960's, Miamians were in for another culinary treat. Thanks to them, we have a continuous feast of all varieties and styles of Cuban and Spanish food. Haitian and other Caribbean cuisines as well as other international favorites have also been added to the menu. As a result, we have the option of "eating our way around the world" in Greater Miami's restaurants and homes.

As we enjoy sampling the cafeteria of delights that is Miami, dessert awaits. It will come when we all sit down together and get to know the cooks.

– Arva Moore Parks

C O N T E N T S

NOTE: Pioneer Recipes are denoted by: Quick and Easy Recipes are denoted by:

INTRODUCTION

About our title, *Biscayne Bights and Breezes*:

Bights are half-moon coves, sheltered bays or curving river inlets along the coastline. They serve as refuge for weary mariners when breezes go from balmy to stormy and they usually offer easy access from the waterline to high ground.

Bights no longer are found on navigation charts of the Biscayne Bay area. They have been integrated into the shoreline by seawalls and bulkheads. However, two most hospitable bights, one in the upper Bay and one to the south, became the nucleus for the growth and development of Greater Miami. Billy Mettair's Bight became Lemon City. Its secure anchorage and overland trails to settlements to the north attracted pioneer families.

Jack's Bight, named for Jolly Jack Peacock, was renamed Cocoanut Grove, and in 1912, Coconut Grove.

The city of Miami, halfway between those bights at the mouth of the Miami River, was a much later idea. When the railroad arrived, Miami reached out and absorbed the older communities.

We have selected a few "bights" from the recipes, records and recollections of our early residents and combined them with some bites, morsels and delicacies, all thoroughly tested, from The Villager's tropical kitchens. Along the way we've added a few breezy bites of southern Florida history.

We hope this book will whet your appetite for our past and for our cuisine, old and new.

The Lighthouse
Key Biscayne
1846

OYSTERS DUNBAR

18 fresh oysters

3 tablespoons flour

1/4 cup (1/2 stick) butter

2 shallots, finely chopped

6 sprigs of parsley, chopped

2 stalks of celery, chopped

2 garlic cloves, pressed

1/4 cup white wine

1/4 cup water

2 teaspoons lemon juice

1 teaspoon Worcestershire sauce

1/8 teaspoon each salt, pepper, cayenne pepper

1 teaspoon each fines herbes and thyme

Clean oysters, open and reserve shells. Dredge oysters in flour and lightly brown in butter. Remove oysters from pan. Sauté shallots, parsley, celery and garlic until translucent. Add oysters, wine, water, lemon juice, Worcestershire sauce and spices.

Cook on low heat for 5 minutes. Return oysters to large half of shell. Reduce liquid over high heat and spoon over each oyster. Garnish with parsley.

Serves 6 or 9

OYSTERS ROBIN

18 to 24 oysters (1 pint), shucked

1 egg yolk

1/2 green pepper, seeded and chopped

2 tablespoons pimento, chopped

1 teaspoon dry mustard

1/2 teaspoon salt

1 tablespoon Worcestershire sauce

1/4 cup mayonnaise

1/4 teaspoon black pepper

1 pound crab meat, cartilage removed

Preheat oven to 350 degrees.

Butter a 9 x 13-inch glass baking dish.

Place oysters in baking dish.

In a medium mixing bowl, combine remaining ingredients except crab meat and mix well. Add crab and stir gently, but thoroughly.

Spread crab mixture over oysters. Bake for 20 minutes. Oysters are cooked when they begin to curl slightly.

Serves 6 to 8

FLORIDIAN SEVICHE

1 pound fillet of pompano, cod or haddock

1 cup lemon juice

1 cup fresh tomatoes, peeled, seeded and chopped

Dash of Tabasco sauce or 4 small hot peppers

1/4 cup vegetable oil

1 teaspoon oregano

1 teaspoon basil

Salt and pepper, to taste

1 small onion, chopped

1 green pepper, sliced

Wash fish and cut into 1/2 or 1-inch strips. Put in a glass or plastic bowl. Pour lemon juice over fish and refrigerate for 2 to 3 hours.

Combine remaining ingredients and let stand to marinate. Add to fish and season to taste. Refrigerate overnight.

Garnish with avocado slices if desired. Some people prefer this dish without the tomatoes and peppers.

Serve as an appetizer or with cocktails.

Serves 4 to 6

PERUVIAN CEVICHE

In Peru, Ecuador and Chile this is also known as cebiche or seviche. In Spain, where it is called escabeche, the fish is lightly poached, covered with hot marinade and refrigerated 12 to 24 hours.

1 pound grouper, sliced into 1/2-inch cubes

1 cup lemon juice

3 tablespoons cilantro, chopped

Parsley, chopped

2 cloves of garlic, minced

1/2 teaspoon black pepper or 1 hot red pepper, minced

1 large red onion, thinly sliced, separated into rings

Put fish in a glass bowl. Add cilantro, parsley, garlic and pepper. Add lemon juice so that fish is covered completely. Marinate in refrigerator for 1 hour or until fish is white.

Garnish with sliced onions.

Serves 8 to 10

Note: This will keep several days in refrigerator. You can substitute shrimp or other shell fish.

THE VIOLET ISLE
Islamorada means 'violet isle' in Spanish. It's surprising that there aren't more names with colors in them since the tropics are so vivid.

Winslow Homer, painting in the 1870's in Florida and the Bahamas, managed to capture in his watercolors the rare range of colors in the sea and sky. He noted how much more brilliant all things looked here than in the North.

Perhaps watercolors are the best medium for expressing the colors. The water from gold through aquamarine to deepest sapphire, and the glorious sunsets and sunrises dazzle the eye.

ISLAMORADA SMOKED FISH PÂTÉ

3 cups smoked fish, skinned, boned and flaked

2 packages (8 ounces each) cream cheese, softened

3 tablespoons fresh lemon juice

2 tablespoons onion, grated

3 tablespoons parsley, chopped

Parsley sprigs (garnish)

Combine cream cheese, lemon juice, and grated onion. Whip until smooth and fluffy. Stir in fish and chopped parsley. Chill for 1 hour. Garnish with parsley. Serve with crackers.

Yields 3-1/2 to 4 cups

Successful deep-sea fishing trip. Florida Keys, 1930

HIALEAH HOLIDAY BRIE EN CROÛTE

1 package (17 ounces) frozen puff pastry

1 cup dried apricots (soak in water for 1 hour)

1 wheel Brie, 2-1/4 pounds (8 inches in diameter)

1/2 cup walnuts, chopped

1 egg yolk

1 tablespoon water

Preheat oven to 425 degrees.

Three hours or more before serving let frozen pastry stand at room temperature to thaw slightly.

One hour before serving unfold 1 sheet of pastry and roll on lightly floured surface to 10 x 13-inch rectangle. Cut a 1-1/2 x 13-inch strip and an 8-1/2-inch diameter circle from rectangle. Repeat with remaining sheet of pastry.

Cut apricots in half. Cut Brie in half to make 2 rounds like a layer cake. Place 1 pastry round on an ungreased cookie sheet. Center bottom half of Brie on it. Layer apricot halves on Brie, sprinkle with walnuts. Top with other half of Brie.

Beat egg yolk with water. Brush side of Brie with the yolk mixture. Wrap the two long pastry strips around the side of Brie and press firmly. Brush pastry strips with remaining yolk mixture. Place other pastry round on top of Brie and press edges of rounds onto pastry strips to seal. (Brushing Brie and pastry with egg yolk keeps pastry from slipping off when hot.)

With tip of knife cut top of pastry into a design, such as a bell for New Year's Eve, a valentine, shamrock, etc. Press deep enough with knife so layers fluff up and flake apart during baking. Bake 30 to 35 minutes until pastry is golden brown. Serve at room temperature or warm. If too hot it will be runny. If made ahead, refrigerate and take out 2 hours before serving.

Serves 24

SPANAKOPETES
(Phyllo Triangles)

2 packages (10 ounces each) frozen chopped spinach, thawed

6 tablespoons olive oil

2 onions, finely chopped

1 pound Feta cheese, crumbled

12 ounces pot cheese

6 eggs

1/2 cup parsley, chopped

2 teaspoons dill weed

1 teaspoon salt

1/2 cup corn flakes, crushed

1 cup (2 sticks) butter, melted

1 package phyllo pastry

Preheat oven to 325 degrees.
12 x 15-inch baking pan, buttered.
Squeeze water from spinach until very dry. Sauté onions in olive oil about 5 minutes, until soft. Add spinach. Mix Feta cheese, pot cheese and eggs. Add parsley, dill weed, salt and corn flakes.
Unwrap phyllo, cut lengthwise into 1-1/2 or 2-inch strips. (Cover with damp towel if you pause for even a few minutes.) Brush each strip with butter, add 1 teaspoon filling and fold flag style into triangles. Press edges firmly. Brush tops with butter.
Bake for 20 to 30 minutes.

Serves 10 to 20

Note: Triangles may be frozen after folding. If frozen do not defrost. Bake immediately until browned and hot.

MEXICAN LAYERED SPREAD

2 packages (8 ounces) cream cheese, softened

1/4 cup milk

1 clove garlic, minced

1 can (16 ounces) refried beans

3 dashes hot pepper sauce

1/2 cup taco sauce

1 large avocado, peeled and cubed

1 medium onion, chopped

1 tablespoon lemon juice

Lettuce leaves, washed and dried

1-1/2 cups Cheddar cheese, shredded

2 medium tomatoes, seeded and chopped

1/2 cup pitted ripe olives, chopped

Tortilla chips

Combine the cream cheese, milk and garlic. Beat on medium speed until smooth. Set aside.
Combine the refried beans, hot pepper sauce and enough taco sauce to make a spreading consistency.
Place the avocado, onion and lemon juice in a blender. Cover and mix thoroughly.
Line a large platter with lettuce leaves. First spread the cream cheese mixture on the lettuce. Then spread the avocado mix evenly on the cream cheese and follow with the bean mixture. Top with shredded Cheddar cheese. Sprinkle with chopped tomatoes and olives.
Cover and chill. Serve with tortilla chips.

Serves 10

CHEESE PUFF PASTRY JALAPEÑO

1 package puff pastry or patty shells

1 brick (8 ounces) Monterey Jack with jalapeño peppers

Preheat oven to 425 degrees.

Thaw pastry and roll to 1/8-inch thickness. Place cheese in the middle of pastry and pull pastry around cheese to seal. Place on teflon coated cookie sheet. Bake until crust is puffed. Brown about 20 minutes. Place on serving tray and serve immediately. Serve taffy pull style.

Serves 8 to 10

. . . .

CHEESE CRESCENTS

6 ounces Bleu cheese

6 ounces Cheddar cheese

12 ounces cream cheese

2 tablespoons onion, grated

1 teaspoon Worcestershire sauce

1/4 cup parsley, chopped

1/2 cup pecans, chopped

The day before, let cheeses stand at room temperature. Blend everything except the last 2 ingredients, and form into crescent shapes. Roll in chopped parsley and pecans. Wrap in plastic and chill in refrigerator overnight.

Serves 10 to 12

NIPPY WAFERS

1 cup flour

1/2 cup (1 stick) butter

1/2 pound sharp Cheddar cheese, grated

1/2 teaspoon cayenne pepper

1/4 teaspoon salt

Preheat oven to 400 degrees.

Mix all ingredients together. Food processors work well. Form into roll about 1-1/2-inches in diameter, wrap in plastic and chill or freeze. Slice into thin rounds and bake on a non-stick cookie sheet for 8 minutes.

If desired, top with pecan halves, crystallized ginger or sesame seeds.

. . . .

BELGIAN ENDIVE WITH YOGURT DIP

2 cups yogurt, plain

2 scallions, chopped

1 teaspoon basil

1/4 teaspoon marjoram

1 teaspoon chervil

Dash Worcestershire sauce

1 medium endive, washed, dried and separated

Mix dip ingredients and refrigerate for 2 days. Stuff endive with dip.

Serves 18 to 24

TROPICAL ART DECO
One square mile of South Miami Beach became this country's first 20th century National Historic District in 1979. It contains more then four hundred Art Deco structures built after the 1926 hurricane leveled most of the area.

The Art Deco style merges the syncopated rhythms of jazz, the glamour of ocean liners, and the romance of the silver screen with the artistic elements of ancient Egyptian and Aztec cultures. The Art Deco of the streamlined industrial North took on a tropical feeling of openness on Miami Beach to capture the ocean breezes and enhance the carefree sun- and sea-filled lifestyle.

Despite some modernization, the wonderful style remains. A walk or drive through the area reveals the many nautical and tropical elements that heighten the romance, fantasy and sense of humor which flavor many of the buildings — flamingos, pelicans, palm trees, fountains, stylized waves and moonlit beaches in bas relief upon façades or etched in glass; verandas, "porthole" windows, racing stripes and cantilevered sunshades called "eyebrows" all set off in sunny yellow, flamingo pink or sea green.

Several hotels along Ocean Drive have been restored to their original stylish elegance and are especially popular with artists, writers and architects. Over a meal or drinks on their verandas or dancing to jazz in the moonlight as cruise ships bob nearby on the ocean waiting for a pilot into port, it's difficult to distinguish where fantasy begins and reality ends.

DECO DILL EGGS AND RED CAVIAR

| Hard-cooked eggs |
| Red Caviar |
| Mayonnaise |
| Butter, melted |
| Salt and pepper, to taste |
| Fresh dill, finely chopped (to taste) |

Cut eggs in half lengthwise and mash yolks with mayonnaise, dill and melted butter until smooth. Stuff into whites of eggs. Chill thoroughly.

At serving time top each egg with small amount of red caviar.

Rejuvenated Art Deco hotel district, Miami Beach

SAMOSAS WITH GARAM MASALA

(Spicy Lamb in Phyllo Triangles)

3 tablespoons oil

1 small onion, finely chopped

3 green chilies, finely chopped

6 cloves garlic, finely chopped

12 pieces ginger, finely chopped

1 pound lamb, minced

1 1/2 tablespoons salt

1/2 teaspoon turmeric

1/2 teaspoon red pepper

1 tablespoon lemon juice

1/4 to 1/2 cup water

1 package egg roll skins or phyllo pastry

2 tablespoons cornstarch mixed with enough water to make paste

3 teaspoons Garam Masala

Oil for frying

Heat oil and sauté onions for 1 minute. Add chilies, garlic, ginger and lamb. Fry for 3 to 4 minutes or until lamb loses its pink color. Drain fat and add Garam Masala mixture. Fry 1 minute. Add 1/4 to 1/2 cup water. Cook until water is absorbed. Cool.

Cut 1 sheet of egg roll or phyllo pastry into fifths. Place 1 tablespoon mixture on each piece and fold like an egg roll or in triangle style. Seal edges closed with cornstarch mixture. When all Samosas are made, deep-fry in hot oil. Drain.

Note: Samosas may be prepared ahead of time, placed on floured wax paper and refrigerated until ready to fry. Freeze on a cookie sheet, store in a sealed bag.

Makes 24 to 36

GARAM MASALA

for Samosas

4 tablespoons black peppercorns

1/2 cup cumin seeds

2 tablespoons garlic

2 tablespoons whole white cardamon

4 to 6 cinnamon sticks

Use whole spices if possible. Bake at 300 to 325 degrees until aroma is evident. Grind in blender until fine consistency. Garam Masala is a type of curry powder.

Makes 24 to 36

BAGNA CAUDA

Bagna Cauda means "hot bath" in Italian. It is served warm and used for dipping vegetables or crusty bread.

2 cups heavy cream

4 cloves of garlic, unpeeled

1/4 cup (1/2 stick) butter, melted

10 flat anchovies, drained and chopped

1 tablespoon fresh parsley, chopped

1/8 teaspoon cayenne pepper

Put cream and garlic in a saucepan and bring to a boil. Lower heat to medium and cook, stirring constantly, until cream has thickened and reduced by half. This takes about 15 minutes. Remove from heat and cool slightly. Discard garlic.

Over low heat add anchovies, butter, parsley and cayenne pepper, stirring constantly.

Serve warm with raw vegetables or cooked artichokes as a first course or appetizer.

Serves 8 to 10

JUDITH SEYMOUR'S CAVIAR AND EGG PIE

8 eggs, hard boiled and mashed

6 tablespoons (3/4 stick) sweet butter, melted

1/4 cup onions, finely chopped

8 ounces sour cream

8 ounces red or black caviar

9-inch pie plate

Mix eggs with melted butter and onions. Press into Pyrex pie plate. Frost the eggs with a heavy layer of sour cream. Refrigerate until set.

Remove from refrigerator. Dot or spread with well drained caviar. Return to refrigerator. Serve well chilled.

Serve as a dip with crackers or rye rounds. Garnish with thin slices of lemon.

Serves 8 to 10

Note: In 1980 an annual scholarship at Florida International University was established by The Villagers as a memorial to our beloved member, Judith Seymour. Since 1985 this scholarship has also been offered at the University of Miami and the University of Florida.

MARINATED ARTICHOKES WITH SOUR CREAM AND CAVIAR

1 can artichoke bottoms

1 cup of your favorite vinaigrette dressing

1 cup sour cream

1 jar red salmon roe (red caviar)

1 jar black caviar

Marinate the artichoke bottoms for a few hours in salad dressing; drain. Fill with sour cream. Top with the caviar.

Serves 8 to 10

. . . .

HOISIN CHICKEN WINGS

24 chicken wings, wing tips discarded

1/3 cup hoisin sauce*

1/3 cup brown sugar

1 tablespoon soy sauce

1 clove garlic, minced

Salt and pepper, to taste

1/4 cup wine (red or white)

Hot pepper, to taste

Marinate wings in mixture at least 1 hour. Broil on both sides until brown. Turn off broiler and bake 10 to 15 minutes at 350 degrees. Baste with marinade.

Serves 15 to 20

*Hoisin sauce is available in gourmet shops.

LILLY'S CHINESE ROAST PORK

1 boneless pork loin (2 to 4 pounds)

1 cup hoisin sauce

12 scallions, ends slashed, placed in ice water to curl (garnish)

Marinate pork overnight in the marinade, covered and refrigerated, turning often.

Roast at 325 degrees for 1-1/2 to 2 hours, basting often with marinade. Brown under broiler. Cool 10 to 15 minutes.

Slice pork very thin. Pour some marinade from the roasting pan over the pork, to keep moist and add flavor. Serve with small rolls, hoisin sauce and scallion curls.

MARINADE

1/4 cup soy sauce

1/2 cup brown sugar

2 cloves garlic, chopped

1 small piece fresh ginger, coarsely chopped

1/4 cup wine, any kind

1/4 cup hoisin sauce

Salt and pepper, to taste

Combine all ingredients and mix well.

Note: Delicious served with Bao (Steamed Buns). (See Index.)

COUNTRY PÂTÉ SANS LIVER

1 pound lean veal, ground

1 pound lean pork, ground

1/4 pound pork fat, ground

1 pound bacon, sliced

1 teaspoon butter, softened

3 tablespoons butter

1 cup onions, finely chopped

2 teaspoons garlic, finely chopped

2 eggs

2-1/2 teaspoons salt

1/2 teaspoon black pepper, freshly ground

1/4 teaspoon allspice

1/2 teaspoon dried thyme

1/4 cup Cognac

2 bay leaves (optional)

Preheat oven to 350 degrees.

Butter 4 x 10-inch pâté dish or casserole.

Pour boiling water over bacon strips and let set for a few minutes. Drain and run cold water over to cool. Pat dry. Line pâté dish with bacon slices, slightly overlapping. Reserve enough for top of pâté. Chill in refrigerator.

Sauté onions in 3 tablespoons butter at high heat until clear, add garlic. Set aside to cool.

Mix ground meat with eggs, seasonings, Cognac and onion mixture. Use hands to mix thoroughly. Pack into pâté dish. Cover with bacon strips. Place bay leaves on top of bacon (optional). Cover with a piece of foil, slightly larger than the dish. Place lid on top of foil.

Set pâté dish in a larger pan on middle shelf of oven. Add hot water to come at least half-way up the sides of the pâté dish. Bake 1-1/2 hours. Remove dish from cooking pan and cool. Remove foil and replace lid. Refrigerate overnight. Serve cold.

Serves 12

Ralph Munroe's boathouse, early headquarters of the Biscayne Bay Yacht Club

POLO PARTY PÂTÉ

1/2 pound chicken livers

1/2 pound veal, ground

1/2 pound lean pork, ground

1 teaspoon allspice

1 tablespoon salt

2 teaspoons rosemary

2 teaspoons thyme

1 teaspoon pepper, freshly ground

1 pinch cayenne pepper

2 cloves garlic, finely chopped

2 medium yellow onions, diced

1/2 cup (1 stick) butter

4 eggs, beaten

Salt pork, thinly sliced to line terrine

1 cup Cognac or any fine brandy

Preheat oven to 325 degrees.

Line terrine or loaf pan with salt pork.

Sauté chicken livers lightly in butter until firm and trim. Reserve liquid.

Use hands to thoroughly mix the veal, pork and spices. Using a blender or processor, chop chicken livers. Add the onions, garlic and reserved liquid. Add veal mixture, eggs and liver purée. Mix in Cognac.

Pour into terrine and cover. Press down to compress pâté. Bake for 1 hour or until it shrinks a little from the sides of the dish.

Remove from oven, cool thoroughly.

Serve sliced with French bread or toast points and sweet midget gherkins.

Serves 20

OF POLO AND PACHYDERMS

Carl Fisher, the flamboyant developer of Miami Beach, was given an elephant named Carl II (which may or may not have been an honor). There are publicity photos of Carl II carrying golf clubs for President Harding or pulling lawn mowers, dragging trees, moving rocks, marching in parades and delighting children at parties.

Every diversion was worth publicizing in an effort to attract "the right people" to spend the winter season on Miami Beach and invest in Fisher's real estate.

He enticed visitors with excellent hotels: the Flamingo, Fleetwood, Nautilus, and King Cole, to name a few. He built tennis courts, swimming pools, golf courses, sports arenas, and invited world class athletes to compete. When he added polo to the list of available activities, he drew the wealthy, high-spirited, younger crowd to his resort.

To do it right, he built the Miami Beach Polo Club and imported professionals with their strings of polo ponies to play exhibitions and compete with the affluent amateurs.

The elephants, Carl II and Rosie, a later addition, were used between chukkers to tramp down the loose turf on the polo field.

Fancy polo picnics are still popular, whether from the "boot" of a Rolls Royce or the tailgate of a station wagon. Champagne, pâté and delicacies served from wicker hampers are traditional polo fare.

"Lay 'em out and keep 'em flat ... then spread 'em. So went the instructions flung at me as a volunteer sandwich maker in the canteen of the 'servicemen's Pier' in 1945. The words pertained to sliced bread.

'The Pier' had a large enclosed area which extended out over the ocean at the south end of Miami Beach on Ocean Drive at Biscayne Street. Miami Beach was packed solid with soldiers in training, housed in commandeered hotels. The 'Pier' offered swimming, fishing, food and a chance to meet a 'young lady' at the evening dances.

"In reference to the 'young ladies' the rules were strict. They had to be 'of age' (I was not, so could only volunteer for daytime work) and 'of decent background.' To preclude any questionable activities, if a hostess left the dance, she could not return again that evening."
– Alicia Brelsford Callander

Note: Before the end of World War II, one-fourth of the Army Air Force Officers, one-fifth of all the enlisted men, 50,000 Navy recruits and platoons of Russian sailors were all trained in the Miami area. Miami was also host to hundreds of German prisoners of war who were imprisoned out west, "in the hinterlands." (That site is presently just south of Dadeland Mall.)

TEA SANDWICH FILLINGS

ROQUEFORT

6 tablespoons Roquefort cheese, mashed

1 tablespoon butter, softened

1 teaspoon sour cream

1 drop lemon juice

CURRIED EGG

6 hard-cooked eggs, chopped

1 tablespoon chutney, chopped

2 tablespoons mayonnaise

2 teaspoons curry powder

1 teaspoon Dijon-style mustard

Salt and pepper, to taste

HERB BUTTER

1/2 cup (1 stick) butter, softened

2 teaspoons tarragon, chopped

2 teaspoons parsley, chopped

2 teaspoons chives, chopped

Season with lemon juice and salt, to taste

PAPRIKA BUTTER

1/2 cup (1 stick) butter, softened

1 tablespoon pimiento, finely chopped

1 teaspoon paprika

Pinch cayenne

Lemon and salt, to taste

TEA SANDWICH FILLINGS CONTINUED

CURRIED TUNA

2 cans (7 ounces) tuna, drained

1 cup mayonnaise

1 teaspoon onion, minced

1 teaspoon curry

1/2 cup (1 stick) butter

Paprika, to taste (garnish)

For each recipe, combine and mix all ingredients until smooth. Spread on thinly sliced buttered bread; crusts removed.

High tea at the Antilla Hotel

NO FOOLIN'
In the early days, each school child had a favorite lunch. Maybe it was a sandwich of homemade bread filled with tomato preserves. Some favored boiled eggs or a boiled sweet potato. They tried to find ways to fool the ants, like using a lard bucket with a lid or by wrapping their lunch in paper and hanging it with string from a tree branch, but it didn't always work.

BACON BIGHTS

1 pound lean bacon

Brown sugar

Preheat oven to 375 degrees.

Place bacon strips cut into thirds or quarters on a rack over a broiler pan lined with foil. Sprinkle brown sugar over each slice and spread to cover evenly.

Bake until crispy. Cool before serving.

Serves 8 to 10

The Biscayne Bay area was and is sailors' country, and sailors have always liked to meet, compete and have parties. The first of many such gatherings began with the Washington's Birthday regatta in 1887. The 15 entries ranged from "a twelve-ton sloop to a Barnegat sneak box." Afterwards, skippers and crews gathered at the Peacock Inn for a festive meal.

Later that year the BBYC was officially formed with Ralph Munroe as commodore and Kirk (no relation) Munroe as secretary. Meetings were held in Commodore Munroe's boat house and later in a new building on pilings in front of his pineapple canning factory.

In the 1890's the BBYC used to stage mock attacks on the Cape Florida lighthouse to "liberate" a big kettle of fish chowder.

Charlie Frow, whose family had been keepers of the Cape Florida lighthouse in the 1870's, worked at the club as lamplighter and dock hand. He learned how to make his excellent fish chowder from Charlie Peacock of the Peacock Inn and for years served as the BBYC official chowder chef. A century later the club members still enjoy the annual chowder party.

CHARLIE FROW'S FISH CHOWDER

1 pound salt pork, skin removed, cut into 1/4-inch cubes

1 pound onions, chopped

1/4 cup green pepper, seeded and chopped

1 quart chicken stock

4 large potatoes, small cubes

1 can tomato soup

4 pounds fresh fish, skin and bones removed, cubed

2 tablespoons butter

2 large cans evaporated milk

Tabasco sauce, to taste

1 bay leaf

1/4 teaspoon thyme

Mace (optional)

In a large kettle brown salt pork then sauté onions and peppers briefly. Add chicken stock, potatoes and tomato soup, cook for 10 minutes. Add fish, cooking slowly until fish is flaky, about 10 minutes. Add butter, milk, and seasonings. Simmer briefly. Add mace if desired.

Serves 12

CONCH AND "ALLIGATOR" SOUP

Okra was called "alligators" by the children growing up in Miami. It was brought to this country from Africa and is beloved throughout the South.

1 pound conch, minced or coarsely ground
2 quarts water
Large beef soup bone with meat
2 tablespoons butter
2 tablespoons flour
1 pound fresh okra, sliced to 1/4-inch rounds
1 large onion, chopped
1 cup corn, fresh or leftover
1/2 pound fresh green beans
3 medium carrots, scrubbed and sliced into pennies
1 large tomato, peeled and chopped
2 Jalapeño peppers, finely chopped
2 sprigs fresh thyme or 1/2 teaspoon dried
Salt, to taste

Place conch in saucepan with beef soup bone and cover with water. Simmer until tender, skimming off top occasionally. Remove meat and discard bone. Reserve meat and conch.

Melt butter in a heavy skillet, add flour and make a roux. When lightly brown, add okra and onion and sauté until wilted.

Add to soup pot with other ingredients, adding water if necessary. Simmer 1 hour, skimming occasionally.

Serve with white rice.

Serves 8 to 10

Fowey Rock Lighthouse, 1878

CHOWDER FOR A CROWD

2 gallons homemade fish stock

6 large baking potatoes, cut into 1/2-inch cubes

5 pounds fresh conch, coarsely chopped

3 quarts tomato sauce

1 cup bacon drippings

2 onions, chopped

1 cup celery, diced

3 green peppers, seeded and diced

3 red bell peppers, seeded and diced

3 tablespoons fresh garlic, minced

4 fresh bay leaves

2 tablespoons fresh basil, finely chopped

2 tablespoons each of thyme, paprika, oregano and crushed red pepper

2 teaspoons each of cayenne, white and black pepper

3 tablespoons salt

2 cups sherry, or to taste

In a large soup pot, bring fish stock to boil, add potatoes. When potatoes are half done, add conch. When potatoes are tender, remove conch and potatoes. Reserve stock.

Heat bacon drippings. Sauté onions, celery, peppers, garlic, herbs and seasonings for 15 minutes.

Add tomato sauce. Reduce heat and cook 15 minutes, stirring frequently. Gradually add reserved stock and blend. Simmer for 1 hour, skimming off fat occasionally. Add potatoes and conch and simmer 1 additional hour.

When ready to serve, stir in sherry; cook 5 minutes.

Serves 20

BISCAYNE BOUILLABAISSE

1 fish head	6 tablespoons olive oil
1/2 pound fresh conch	1-1/2 cups onion, chopped
1 quart clam juice or fish stock	1/4 teaspoon fennel seed
2 quarts water	1/4 teaspoon thyme

4 cloves garlic, peeled and crushed

1/4 teaspoon saffron threads, crushed

1/2 teaspoon orange zest

3/4 teaspoon salt

Pinch white pepper

8 tomatoes, peeled and quartered or 1 can (28 ounces) crushed tomatoes

12 ounces beer

3 Florida lobster tails in shells, scrubbed

1 dozen small clams in the shell, scrubbed

1 pound grouper, boned, cut into large pieces

1 pound snapper, boned, cut into large pieces

1/2 pound medium shrimp, peeled, deveined

1/2 pound bay scallops

Soak conch in clam juice or stock for 2 hours to tenderize. Drain, reserving liquid; pound conch.

In a very large soup pot, cook fish head and conch in stock and water for 2 hours. Strain, reserving stock. Chop conch.

Sauté onion and garlic in olive oil until golden and tender. Add herbs, zest, salt, pepper, tomatoes and beer. Simmer 15 minutes. Add to stock pot. Return stock to a boil.

Add lobster tails and conch, reduce heat and simmer 5 minutes.

Add clams and fish pieces and simmer 5 minutes.

Add shrimp and scallops and simmer 5 minutes.

Shell the lobsters, cut into large chunks. Ladle broth into deep soup bowls, add seafood. Serve with crusty bread and a crisp salad.

Serves 16 to 18

"My recipe for bouillabaisse came from the Herald. It was written around 1920 by Mrs. Charlie Thompson, the wife of the famous fishing guide who was Captain of Mr. Mellon's yacht. They came to Biscayne Bay every winter from New York.

"You know this dish came originally from the Mediterranean, mainly from Marseille in France. The title means 'low-boiled.' It's a very old dish.

"Bouillabaisse is a very accommodating soup. You can do a lot of things with it. You can add sherry if you like. Put some buttered French bread or croutons in a soup plate and serve it. I used to make it for a big party, a big kettle full. There was no bother about serving that sort of thing. Everybody would just come in with a bowl and a spoon." – Marjorie Stoneman Douglas

ALL IN GOOD FUN

Richard Carney first came to this area as a foreman, supervising workmen planting coconuts on sixty-five miles of barrier islands from Key Biscayne northward up Miami Beach to Jupiter Inlet. That involved hacking, gouging and chopping through tough scrub, dense mangroves and countless oversized mosquitoes and undersized sandflies (called "flying teeth" in the Bahamas). The project was ultimately unsuccessful. Rabbits ate the fresh young shoots of the coconut plants.

Carney dismantled his shack and floated it over to Coconut Grove where he became well known as a likeable, hard working adventurer, excellent sailor ... and noted prankster.

One bit of mischief made its way into Owen Wister's book, The Virginian. One night during a Housekeeper's Club party, he slipped into the room where the guests' children were sleeping. He shifted them around and exchanged boys' clothes for girls.' Later that night the guests gathered their sleeping bundles and sailed home. Just imagine the uproar! And there was the time he painted stripes on a neighbor's mule, confusing both the man and the animal.

"Captain" Carney and "Commodore" Munroe were the best of friends, sharing long, difficult and often exciting sailing trips. Their names are equally important in the log books of the Biscayne Bay Yacht Club.

CAPTAIN CARNEY'S 1920 GROUPER CHOWDER

1/2 cup salt pork, cut into fine cubes

2 medium carrots, finely chopped

1 onion, finely chopped

1 can (12 ounces) tomatoes, broken up

1/2 green pepper, diced

2 cups raw potatoes, cubed

1 tablespoon Worcestershire sauce

1 pound grouper, cubed

1 quart milk

Parsley, chopped (garnish)

Render salt pork and cook all ingredients except fish and milk on low heat for 20 minutes. Add fish and stir gently. Cook slowly for 30 minutes until fish is tender.

Add milk and continue to heat; do not boil. Sprinkle with fresh chopped parsley.

Serves 8

Making chowder at the yacht club

CLASSIC CIOPPINO

3/4 cup onions, chopped

2 cloves garlic, minced

3/4 cup green peppers, chopped

1/3 cup olive oil, finest quality

1 can (1 pound 13 ounces) tomatoes, broken up

1 cup dry red wine

1 bay leaf

1 teaspoon marjoram, ground

1 teaspoon leaf basil, crumbled

1/2 teaspoon leaf thyme, crumbled

3 tablespoons parsley, chopped

2 teaspoons salt

1/4 teaspoon pepper

3 pounds sea bass or other firm-fleshed fish, cut up

1 lobster (2 1/2 pounds), cut up

1 pound fresh shrimp, shelled and deveined

18 little neck clams or 12 mussels, well scrubbed

In a large soup pot, sauté onion, garlic and green pepper in hot oil until tender. Add tomatoes, wine, bay leaf, marjoram, basil, thyme and parsley. Cover and simmer for 1 hour.

Add salt, pepper, fish, lobster and shrimp. Cook for 10 minutes. Do not stir.

Add clams or mussels and cook just until shells open.

Serve at once with toasted Italian bread and red or white wine.

Serves 12 to 14

Venetian Pool, Coral Gables

23

QUICK FISH STOCK

2 cups bottled clam juice

1 cup water

1 cup dry white wine

1 onion, sliced

1 carrot, sliced

2 stalks celery, sliced

2 sprigs parsley

1 bay leaf

1/2 teaspoon dried thyme

Salt and white pepper, to taste

Place all ingredients in a heavy saucepan, bring to a boil, turn down heat and simmer 30 minutes. Strain through fine sieve.

Conch shell and shrimp boat

BAY SHRIMP SOUP

12 ounces tomato juice

4 cups chicken or shrimp stock

1/3 cup dry white wine

1/2 cup tomatoes, peeled and diced

1/3 cup onions, chopped

1/2 cup celery, chopped

1/4 teaspoon black pepper, coarsely ground

1-1/2 teaspoons garlic, minced

1 teaspoon sweet basil

1/4 teaspoon tarragon

1/8 teaspoon paprika

1 bay leaf

Tabasco sauce, to taste

1 pound small raw shrimp, peeled and deveined

In a large soup pot, combine all ingredients except shrimp and bring to boil. Reduce heat; simmer 1/2 hour.

Add shrimp 5 minutes before serving. As soon as they are pink and firm, soup is ready. Serve with French bread.

Serves 4 to 6

EASY CONCH CHOWDER

1 quart water

1 pound conch, finely chopped or ground

3/4 cup potatoes, diced

4 ounces bacon or salt pork, diced

1/2 cup onions, chopped

1/2 cup celery, chopped

1/2 cup sweet red peppers, chopped

2 tablespoons flour

2 tomatoes, chopped

1/2 teaspoon salt

1/2 teaspoon thyme

1/4 teaspoon hot pepper sauce

Sherry, to taste

In a large soup pot, boil water. Add conch and potatoes and let simmer 15 minutes. Remove conch and potatoes. Reserve broth.

Fry bacon, onions, celery and peppers for 5 minutes over medium heat. Gradually add flour, tomatoes, salt, thyme and hot pepper sauce and stir until smooth. Blend thoroughly into broth. Add conch and potatoes to broth and simmer 30 minutes. Add additional water if necessary.

Let stand for a few minutes before serving.

Serves 6 to 8

UPPER-CRUST ONION SOUP

6 tablespoons butter

2 large Spanish onions, thinly sliced

2 quarts beef stock

6 slices French bread

1/2 pound Gruyère or Swiss cheese, grated

6 egg yolks, beaten

6 ounces Port wine

Salt and pepper, to taste

Melt 2 tablespoons butter in a saucepan and cook onions until tender but not brown. Add beef stock, salt and pepper. Simmer 15 minutes over medium heat.

Purée hot soup in a food processor or blender.

In a skillet, brown bread on both sides in remaining butter.

Combine egg yolks and wine and put in a bowl. Set aside.

When serving put 1 slice browned bread in a soup bowl, cover with broth, sprinkle with cheese and place under the broiler for 1 minute. Remove from broiler, cut crust of cheese with a tablespoon and pour in 1/4 cup of the egg/wine mixture.

Serves 6 to 8

BUCCANEERS AND PRIVATEERS

The huge treasure fleets sailing up the east coast of Florida provided a rich source of salvage as well as human captives. It didn't take long for pirates to join the grim game.

The Caribbean was a hotbed of some of the most daring outlaws the world has ever known. They liked to call themselves "buccaneers." In the 17th and 18th centuries the word entered our vocabulary with a sinister meaning.

Along the Spanish coast of America those pirates were of every nationality. Some have gone down in history as either national heroes, as in the case of Sir Francis Drake, or as arch criminals – depending on whose ship was captured. Even when the era of great treasure fleets came to an end in the 17th century, pirates still preyed on coastal shipping.

During wars, however, another category of militant seafarer arrived ... the privateers. They were ships of war, equipped and operated by one or more groups of persons, generally patriotic, adventurous or greedy.

They were licensed to seize and plunder enemy vessels. It is possible that some captains with imperfect eyesight or a short attention span would attack a "friendly" vessel, but by the time it was dismasted and in chaos it was too late to apologize.

SPANISH BEAN SOUP

1/4 pound garbanzo beans

1 tablespoon salt

1/2 pound ham, cut into chunks

2 quarts water

1/4 pound salt pork or bacon, rendered

1 onion, chopped

3 medium potatoes, peeled and quartered

2 chorizos (Spanish sausage), sliced, cooked

In a soup pot, wash beans thoroughly; soak overnight with 1 tablespoon salt and enough water to cover. Next morning, drain beans, add 2 quarts water and ham. Simmer 45 minutes.

Sauté salt pork and onions and add to beans. Add potatoes and cook 30 to 45 minutes, then add sliced sausage.

Serve hot with crusty bread and salad.

Serves 4 to 6

1750 French map of Louisiana

CHILLED CREAM OF AVOCADO SOUP

4 avocados

2 cups chicken broth

2 teaspoons lime juice

3/4 teaspoon salt

1/4 teaspoon garlic, minced (or to taste)

2 cups half and half or heavy cream

Purée the first 5 ingredients. Combine with cream and chill thoroughly. Garnish with fresh avocado slices.

Hot pepper sauce, cumin, chopped tomatoes or finely shredded tortillas may be added.

Serves 4

• •

COOL CANTALOUPE SOUP

A refreshing first course or a delightfully light dessert.

1 large cantaloupe, peeled, seeded and chopped

1 lime, juiced

1/2 orange, juiced

1 cup cream

1 tablespoon honey

1/2 cup dry white wine

Lime, thinly sliced (garnish)

Purée cantaloupe in food processor with lime and orange juice. Add cream, honey and white wine that has been reduced 1/2 by cooking over medium heat.

Chill the soup for several hours and serve in chilled cups. Float a thin slice of lime on top of each cup.

Serves 4

CURRIED CONSOMMÉ COOLER

2 cans beef consommé, gelatin added

1 package (8 ounces) cream cheese, softened

1/8 teaspoon curry powder

Cherry tomatoes, parsley or dill (garnish)

Heat 1 can beef consommé to boiling. Add cream cheese and stir until melted. Add curry powder. Pour into sherbet dishes, chill until set.

Heat other can of consommé to liquid consistency. Pour 1/2 inch over top of cold soup and chill.

Garnish with cherry tomato, parsley or dill.

Serves 6

• •

CHILLED CREAM OF CUCUMBER SOUP

4 medium cucumbers, peeled, seeded, sliced

1 small onion, sliced

1 cup tomato juice

1 tablespoon tomato paste

1 cup strong chicken stock

1 quart sour cream

4 tablespoons dry sherry

Salt and black pepper, freshly ground (to taste)

Basil leaves (garnish)

Purée cucumbers, onions, tomato juice and tomato paste. Add chicken stock, sour cream and sherry; blend until smooth. Season with salt and pepper.

Refrigerate for 2 hours or more.

Garnish each serving with a fresh basil leaf.

Serves 6 to 8

COLD BILLI-BI SOUP

(Mussel Soup)

5 pounds mussels, scrubbed

1 clove garlic, crushed with skin

3/4 cup onion, chopped

1/2 cup (8 to 10) shallots, chopped

1 tablespoon sweet butter

2 cups very dry white wine

1 bay leaf, crushed

1/2 teaspoon fresh thyme, crushed

1/2 cup parsley, coarsely chopped

2 teaspoons salt

1 teaspoon black pepper, freshly ground

2 cups heavy cream

2 egg yolks

Place all ingredients except cream, egg yolks and fresh herbs in a large soup pot. (Do not use aluminum as it discolors the soup.) Bring to a rolling boil, covered, stirring for 1 to 2 minutes until mussels open and liquid comes out.

Combine 1/2 cup heavy cream with the egg yolks and fresh herbs in a bowl and set aside.

Add the remaining cream to the pot; bring mixture to a boil. Remove from heat and strain mixture through a large colander into a bowl. Remove the mussels and save for later use. Return all liquids to pot.

Add 1 cup of the hot liquid, a little at a time, to the cream/egg yolk mixture, whisking continuously to prevent yolks from curdling. Return to pot, continuing to whisk until mixture coats the whisk. Pour through a fine strainer and cool, stirring to prevent a skin from forming. Refrigerate until cold and serve.

Yields 2 quarts
Serves 6 to 8

Note: The mussels are not served in this soup. They can be served separately in olive oil and parsley or in a sour cream sauce.

BRICKELL BROCCOLI BISQUE

5 stalks of fresh broccoli, trimmed, chopped

3-1/2 cups chicken broth, fresh or canned

1 medium onion, quartered

2 tablespoons butter

1/2 tablespoon curry powder

1 tablespoon salt

Dash of pepper

2 tablespoons lime juice

Broccoli florets

Lemon slices (garnish)

Sour cream (garnish)

Chives (garnish)

Peanuts (optional)

In large saucepan, boil broth. Add broccoli, onion, butter, curry powder, salt and pepper. Reduce heat and simmer covered for 8 to 12 minutes or until tender.

Place 1/2 of mixture in blender and blend until smooth. Repeat. Stir in lime juice. Cover and refrigerate for at least 4 hours.

At serving time, place several broccoli florets into small bowls, cover with the chilled bisque, and garnish with lemon slices, sour cream and chives.

Serves 4 to 6

B RICKELL'S TRADING POST

William Brickell established a trading post in the 1870's at the mouth of the Miami River. It supplied such diverse pioneer needs as flour, toothache drops, kerosene and shoes. It was also the local post office.

The Seminole Indians gave Mr. Brickell most of his business. Nearly every day they came over the rapids of the Miami River in cypress dugout canoes from their camps at the edge of the Everglades. They brought deer, otter and alligator skins, coontie, pumpkins, sweet potatoes and egret plumes for "barter." They actually insisted upon receiving silver coins which they then paid back coin-by-coin as they selected a few staples such as sugar and other items which caught their eye.

Especially popular were brightly colored calicoes, red and turquoise beads, alarm clocks and foot-pedal sewing machines. Charitable Christian ladies gave sewing lessons and the Indians' native buckskin dress soon gave way to brightly colored calico clothing, often with several patchwork patterns in one garment.

An Indian woman's prosperity and standing in her community was measured by her necklaces which consisted of yards and yards of beads and silver coins, sometimes weighing as much as 25 pounds and reaching from her shoulder bone to her ear tip.

FRESCO MANGO TANGO

On a hot summer day, this is a wonderful first course for a luncheon or as a dessert with your favorite cake.

2 cups water

1 cup sugar

2 sticks cinnamon

2 teaspoons whole cloves

1/3 cup arrowroot

3 cups dry white wine

6 pounds very ripe Hayden mangos, peeled, pitted and sliced

1/2 cup heavy cream

2 tablespoons sugar

1/2 cup sour cream

1 cup fresh raspberries or blueberries (garnish)

Place the water, sugar, cinnamon and cloves in a saucepan and bring to a boil. Cover and simmer for 30 minutes. Mixture should become slightly thick and syrupy.

Combine the arrowroot with the wine and add to the spice mixture, stirring until blended. Bring to a rolling boil and set aside to cool.

Purée 1/2 of the mangos in food processor and add to syrup. Refrigerate until cold.

Just before serving, whip heavy cream with the sugar and fold into chilled soup. Fold in sour cream and remaining mangos. Garnish with raspberries or blueberries.

Serves 8

Note: Peaches may be substituted for mangos.

COLD CREAM OF ZUCCHINI SOUP

3 pounds (about 8 to 10) zucchini, scrubbed, thinly sliced

1 cup onions, chopped

1 clove garlic, pressed

1 teaspoon curry powder

3 cups chicken stock

2 cups heavy cream

Salt and white pepper, to taste

Watercress (garnish)

Parboil 1 sliced zucchini 2 minutes; chill in cold water. Drain and set aside.

Cook remaining zucchini with onion, garlic, curry powder and stock in a large soup pot. Bring to a boil, cover and simmer 40 minutes.

Purée ingredients in a food processor or blender, add cream, stir in the zucchini slices. Garnish with watercress. This soup may be served hot or cold.

Serves 8

"MICCO," designed by Munroe

APPLE PUFFED PANCAKE

This is splendid for a Sunday morning brunch.

6 eggs

1-1/2 cups milk

1 cup all-purpose flour

3 tablespoons granulated sugar

1 teaspoon vanilla extract

1/2 teaspoon salt

1/4 teaspoon cinnamon

1/4 pound (1 stick) butter

2 apples, peeled, thinly sliced

2 to 3 tablespoons brown sugar

Preheat oven to 425 degrees.

In a blender or large bowl, mix eggs, milk, flour, sugar, vanilla, salt and cinnamon until blended. If using a mixer, batter will remain slightly lumpy.

In oven, melt butter in a 12-inch fluted porcelain quiche dish or 9 x 13-inch baking dish. Add apple slices to dish. Return to oven until butter sizzles. Do not let brown.

Remove dish from oven and immediately pour batter over apples. Sprinkle with brown sugar. Bake in middle of oven 30 minutes or until puffed and brown. Serve immediately.

Serves 6 to 8

MONKEY BREAD
(Cinnamon Bubble Coffee Cake)

Monkey bread is one of President Reagan's favorites.

2 packages active dry yeast

1/2 cup warm water

1/2 cup milk, scalded

1/2 cup shortening

1/2 cup white sugar

1 teaspoon salt

4 to 4-1/2 cups flour

2 eggs, beaten

1/4 cup (1/2 stick) butter, melted

1/2 cup brown sugar

1/2 cup white sugar

1-1/2 teaspoons cinnamon

Preheat oven to 350 degrees.

Thoroughly butter a 10-inch tube pan.

Dissolve yeast in water with a pinch of sugar.

Combine milk, shortening, sugar and salt in large mixing bowl. Cool to lukewarm. Add 1 cup flour and beat well. Add yeast mixture and eggs. Beat until smooth. Mix in enough remaining flour to make a soft dough.

Knead on lightly floured surface 8 to 10 minutes. Place in greased bowl, turning once to grease surface. Cover, let rise until double, about 1 hour. Punch down. Cover and let rest 10 minutes.

Divide dough into 24 equal pieces. Shape into balls. Mix brown and white sugar and cinnamon. Roll each ball in melted butter then in sugar mixture. Arrange in pan. Sprinkle with any remaining sugar mixture. Let rise until double, about 1 hour.

Bake for 35 to 40 minutes. Cool in pan 15 to 20 minutes. Invert on rack and remove pan.

Makes 20 to 24

Large ketch on Biscayne Bay

33

MAGIC CITY MANGO BREAD

2 cups flour

2 teaspoons cinnamon

2 teaspoons baking soda

3/4 cup white sugar

3/4 cup brown sugar

1/2 teaspoon salt

1 cup coconut, flaked

3 eggs, slightly beaten

1 teaspoon vanilla

1 cup salad oil

2 cups mango, diced

1/2 cup nuts, chopped

1/2 cup raisins

Preheat oven to 350 degrees.

Butter two 5 x 9-inch bread pans.

Stir together flour, cinnamon, baking soda, sugar and salt. Add other ingredients and mix.

Pour into bread pans and bake for 55 minutes.

Makes 2 loaves

COCONUT PLANTATION BREAD

3 cups all-purpose flour, sifted

1 tablespoon baking powder

1/2 teaspoon salt

1 cup sugar

1 cup coconut, shredded

1 egg, beaten

1 cup milk

1 teaspoon vanilla extract

Preheat oven to 325 degrees.

Butter a 5 x 9-inch loaf pan.

Sift dry ingredients, add coconut and mix thoroughly. Combine liquid ingredients and dry ingredients. Blend carefully. Let stand for 20 minutes.

Pour into loaf pan. Bake for 45 to 50 minutes.

Makes 1 loaf

Note: Do not skip the step calling for 20 minutes of setting before putting in the oven. If a chewy texture is desired bake for 60 minutes.

A PIONEER PLANTER
Among the first people to understand and take advantage of the Miami area's unique combination of natural blessings was Richard Fitzpatrick, a plantation-born gentleman from South Carolina who had become one of Key West's outstanding citizens.

In the 1830's he saw an ad in the Key West Register which read: "FOR SALE, A VALUABLE TRACT OF LAND NEAR CAPE FLORIDA. Situated on the Miami River. The LAND is very good and will produce Sugar Cane or Sea-Island Cotton, equal, if not superior to any other part of the Territory. There is at present a number of bearing Banana and Lime Trees, and the fruit is inferior to none raised in the Island of Cuba. The forest growth consists principally of Live Oak, Red Bay and Dog Wood. Any person desirous of purchasing valuable plantation will do well to visit the Land. – JAMES EGAN"

Richard Fitzpatrick responded and bought 640 acres for $400. Adding to his initial investment, he soon acquired four square miles along the river and one square mile of what is now Ft. Lauderdale. With the aid of 60 slaves and two overseers, he turned his holdings into a model plantation, producing sugar cane, corn, cotton, limes, coconuts, sweet potatoes and pumpkins.

Unfortunately, the bright future was dimmed by the outbreak of the first Seminole War in 1835, thus ending the first major settlement of what is now downtown Miami.

PANCAKES Á L'ORANGE WITH SUNSHINE SYRUP

2 egg yolks

1/2 teaspoon salt

2 tablespoons Florida honey

2 cups orange sections, finely chopped

1 cup flour, sifted

1/2 teaspoon baking powder

2 egg whites, stiffly beaten

Butter and oil for frying

Beat the egg yolks, salt and honey together. Stir in orange sections, flour, and baking powder. Fold in beaten egg whites.

Heat butter and oil to cover bottom of skillet. Drop batter by tablespoons into skillet and brown on both sides.

Serves 4

SUNSHINE SYRUP

1/2 pound (2 sticks) butter, melted

1 cup all-purpose flour

1 quart fresh orange juice, heated

3/4 cup sugar

1/4 cup orange peel, cut into julienne

Melt butter in saucepan. While stirring slowly add flour. Cook on medium low for 5 minutes.

Add heated orange juice and stir briskly until sauce simmers. Add sugar and orange peel. Simmer 5 minutes more.

Makes 1 quart

BAO

(Steamed Buns)

1 cup milk

1/2 cup sugar

2 teaspoons salt

3/4 cup cold water

1/2 cup warm water, 105 to 115 degrees

2 teaspoons sugar

2 teaspoons or 2/3 package yeast

7-1/2 cups flour

2 eggs, beaten

Waxed paper squares

Mix first 4 ingredients and scald in small saucepan and let cool.

Dissolve sugar and yeast in warm water and let set for 15 minutes.

Add yeast mixture and eggs to milk mixture, then add enough flour to make a kneadable dough. Knead and let rise 2 hours.

Punch down and roll into a small cylinder. Pinch or cut off small pieces and roll into flat rounds 2 to 3 inches in diameter. Oil 1 side and fold half over. Put waxed paper between rolls and place into steamer. Let rise for 2 hours.

Steam 20 minutes, turn off the heat and let them rest a few minutes before serving.

At this point the buns can be frozen. When ready to serve, steam them again for 15 to 20 minutes.

Serves 30 as an appetizer or 6 to 8 as main course

Note: Delicious served with Lilly's Chinese Roast Pork. (See Index.)

BANANA BREAD

1 cup sugar

1/2 cup butter

3 medium ripe bananas, mashed

1 teaspoon baking soda

4 tablespoons buttermilk, or regular milk with a few drops of vinegar

2 eggs, beaten

2 cups flour, sifted

1/2 cup nuts

1/4 teaspoon salt

Preheat oven to 350 degrees.

Grease and flour 5 x 9-inch loaf pan.

Cream sugar and butter, add bananas. Dissolve baking soda in the buttermilk. Add beaten eggs and buttermilk mixture to the banana mixture. Add flour, nuts and salt and mix thoroughly.

Bake for about 35 minutes.

Makes 1 large loaf

Note: For an interesting variation, instead of bananas you can substitute 1/2 teaspoon cinnamon and 1 cup Calamondin Purée. (See Index).

CRANBERRY LOAF

1 cup fresh cranberries, chopped

2 eggs, well beaten

1 cup sugar

1 teaspoon salt

1/2 cup vegetable oil

1-1/2 cups flour, sifted

1 teaspoon soda

Preheat oven to 350 degrees.

Grease a 5 x 9-inch loaf pan.

In blender or food processor mix cranberries, sugar and eggs until puréed. Add dry ingredients and oil.

Bake in loaf pan for 1 hour or until toothpick comes out of the center clean.

Makes 1 loaf

NDERSON'S CORNER GENERAL STORE

This humble frame structure in South Dade County was built in 1911 as a general store catering to loggers and farmers in the area. That part of the country was once thickly wooded and had been known as "The Hunting Grounds" until the arrival of the railroad in 1898 made extensive lumbering feasible.

Today the area, now known as The Redlands, produces many of our famous winter crops, including tomatoes, beans, squash, limes and strawberries, which are shipped to northern markets.

When Anderson's Corner was first built it saved local residents a lot of travel time. It eliminated an all-day trip by mule and wagon to the little port of Cutler on Biscayne Bay and then a long sail to Miami for supplies.

Will Anderson, who lived above the store with his wife and step-children, sold everything from "dynamite to lace" and the store also served as a meeting place and social hall for the homesteaders.

The sturdy old building, constructed by shipwrights out of nearly indestructible Dade County pine, was saved by preservationists led by The Villagers in 1976. It was later sold to private interests for use as a restaurant.

ANDERSON'S CORNER AVOCADO BREAD

2 cups sugar

3 eggs

1 teaspoon vanilla

1 cup ripe avocado, mashed

1/4 cup vegetable oil

3 cups all-purpose flour, sifted

1 teaspoon baking soda

1 teaspoon baking powder

1/4 teaspoon cinnamon

1 teaspoon salt

1/2 cup water

1-1/2 cups walnuts, chopped

Preheat oven to 350 degrees.

Grease and flour two 5 x 9-inch loaf pans.

Combine sugar, eggs, vanilla. Beat well. Add avocado and oil, blend until smooth. Gradually add sifted dry ingredients. Blend at medium speed, until smooth. Add water. Stir in chopped nuts.

Pour into loaf pans and bake for 50 to 55 minutes. Bread is done when toothpick inserted in center comes out clean.

Makes 2 large or 7 small loaves

Note: Bake in 7 miniature loaf pans reducing baking time to 35 minutes. They make wonderful gifts.

SPICED PUMPKIN BREAD

4 cups flour

2 teaspoons baking soda

1/2 teaspoon baking powder

1 teaspoon cinnamon, ground

1 teaspoon cloves, ground

1 teaspoon salt

8 tablespoons butter, softened

2-1/2 cups sugar

4 eggs

2 cups fresh or canned pumpkin, puréed

1/2 cup plus 1 tablespoon water

1/2 cup seedless raisins, finely chopped

1/2 cup black walnuts or pecans, chopped

8 ounces cream cheese, whipped

Preheat oven to 350 degrees.

Using 2 tablespoons butter, thoroughly butter and flour two 5 x 9-inch loaf pans.

Sift together flour, baking soda, baking powder, cinnamon, cloves and salt. In a mixing bowl, cream 6 tablespoons butter and sugar.

Beat eggs into the sugar mixture, one at a time. Stir in puréed pumpkin. Add flour mixture, 1 cup at a time, and water, 3 tablespoons at a time. Beat well after each addition. Stir in nuts.

Bake in the middle of the oven for 50 to 60 minutes or until done.

Serve with cream cheese whipped with a bit of cream to soften.

Makes 2 loaves

PIONEER PRUNE BREAD

1 cup prunes

1 cup milk

3 tablespoons shortening

1/2 cup prune juice

4 teaspoons sugar

2 tablespoons molasses

2 teaspoons salt

2 packages dry yeast

1/2 cup lukewarm water (105 to 115 degrees)

2 cups whole-grain or graham flour

5-1/2 cups white flour, approximately

Preheat oven to 375 degrees.

Soak the prunes in cold water overnight and cook until soft. Remove stones and cut into small pieces. (Non-pioneers can use pitted prunes.)

Scald the milk and add shortening, prune juice, sugar, molasses and salt. When milk mixture is lukewarm, add yeast which has been softened in warm water. Add graham flour, prunes and enough white flour to make a stiff dough.

Knead until smooth and let rise until doubled in bulk. Punch down, shape into 2 loaves, and let double in size again.

Bake 1 hour in 375 degree oven.

Makes 2 medium loaves

The "Egret" at Bear Cut, 1886

HONEY WHOLE WHEAT BREAD

This food processor recipe is wholesome and delicious.

1/4 to 1/2 cup warm water

3 tablespoons honey

1 package active dry yeast

2 cups unbleached white flour

3/4 cup whole wheat flour

1/4 cup instant nonfat dry milk

2 tablespoons butter

1 teaspoon salt

1 egg

Preheat oven to 375 degrees.

Butter a 4 x 8-inch loaf pan.

Combine 1/4 cup water, 1 tablespoon honey and yeast. Stir to dissolve yeast; let stand until bubbly, about 5 minutes.

Fit food processor with steel blade. Measure flours, dry milk, butter, remaining 2 tablespoons honey, and salt into work bowl. Process until mixed, about 10 seconds. Add yeast mixture and egg to flour mixture. Process until blended, about 10 seconds.

Very slowly through the feed tube add just enough remaining water so dough forms a ball that cleans the sides of the bowl. Process until ball turns around bowl about 60 times.

Turn dough out of work bowl. Shape into ball and place in lightly greased bowl, turning to grease all sides. Cover loosely with plastic wrap and let stand in warm place until doubled, about 1 hour.

Punch dough down. Shape into loaf and place in pan. Let rise again until almost doubled in bulk, about 45 minutes.

Brush top of loaf with egg wash, if desired. Bake until bread sounds hollow when tapped, 25 to 30 minutes. Remove from pan immediately. Cool on wire rack.

Makes 1 loaf

CHAPATI DOUGH PURIS
(Indian Bread Puffs)

2 cups wheat pastry flour or 1 cup each of whole wheat flour and unbleached white flour

2 tablespoons vegetable oil

1/2 teaspoon salt

1/2 cup water (perhaps a little more)

Oil for deep frying

Mix flours and salt. Place in large bowl. Add 2 tablespoons oil. Using hands, work oil into flour until thoroughly mixed. Add water, small amounts at a time, using hands to blend. Dough will eventually form a ball.

Knead the dough for at least 10 minutes. The finished dough should be slightly sticky but firm. Put drops of water on the dough so it will not dry out, cover. Let it rest at least 30 minutes.

Pull off pieces of dough the size of ping pong balls and roll in mixture of white and wheat flour. Roll out very thin or pat with your hand. Cut into 2-inch circles or squares.

Heat oil to 365 degrees. Place flattened dough in the oil and immediately start hitting it with a slotted spoon. This will make dough puff. When dough puffs turn over for a moment, remove and drain on paper towels.

Serve immediately with curried food.

Makes about 2 dozen

Note: The dough is Chapati dough but each piece is called a puri or poori. It can be made in the morning and used in the evening. Leftovers keep well in the refrigerator for 1 week.

BARREL BREAD
In olden days, most homes had a hundred pound barrel of flour to last through the winter. Bread was mixed right in the barrel by making a well in the flour with your fist, dumping in liquid and then stirring until a ball was formed.

"Cero," a 62-foot ketch designed by Munroe

NO EGGS
Pioneer families in South Florida often were confronted with shortages of eggs because of the scarcity of chickens. What a problem this was for the average family accustomed to eating pancakes, bread, corn bread and muffins on a daily basis. When eggs were unavailable, an adequate replacement was discovered by innovative pioneer cooks. They would substitute a couple of tablespoons of thick cooked corn meal mush or hominy grits for each egg called for in the recipe.

Another solution was to use the once abundant eggs of "loggerhead" and green turtles, now endangered and protected by law. However, the whites of the egg would never congeal and they were very difficult to beat into other ingredients. After boiling them for 1-1/2 hours the whites would become only slightly thickened.

VILLAGERS' SPOON BREAD

| 1 cup white water-ground corn meal |
| 4 cups milk |
| 3 tablespoons butter, melted |
| 1/2 teaspoon salt |
| 4 eggs, well beaten |

Preheat oven to 400 degrees.

Grease 2 quart casserole or baking pan.

Blend the corn meal with 1 cup milk. Stir in remaining milk. Cook and stir over moderate heat until the mixture thickens. Add melted butter and salt. Fold in eggs.

Pour into baking pan or casserole and bake for 25 to 30 minutes. Spoon out servings.

Serves 6 to 8

The pinelands of Homestead Country. (Romer Collection)

HOMESTEAD HUSH PUPPIES

2 cups yellow corn meal

1 cup self-rising flour

1 large onion, finely chopped

1/2 large green pepper, seeded and finely chopped (optional)

2 eggs

1 teaspoon salt

1 teaspoon sugar (optional)

2 cups milk or buttermilk

Combination of vegetable oil and bacon fat for deep frying

Mix first 8 ingredients in a bowl.

Heat oil to 375 degrees in deep fat fryer.

Using a tablespoon, pick up less than a spoonful of mixture. Drop the batter into deep fat. Cook until golden brown.

Makes 20 to 24

The first train into Miami, April 22, 1896 (Romer Collection)

"HOMESTEAD COUNTRY" In 1903 when the Florida East Coast Railroad was laying out the rails in South Florida, the Homestead area was still unbroken wilderness. William Alfred King, the section foreman, moved his work camp down from Perrine and constructed the first permanent buildings: the depot, offices for the station agent and a tool shed. The workers camped in portable buildings which were torn down as each section of the rails was laid, moved on flat cars to the end of the completed track and set up again. Since there was no name for the end of the line the cars carrying supplies and building materials were labeled in chalk "Homestead Country." Engineers mapping the area dropped the word "country" and labeled the work camp "Homestead."

PUMPKIN FRY BREAD

2 cups self-rising flour

1 can (16 ounces) pumpkin

3/4 cup sugar

Stir together flour, pumpkin and sugar.

Chill until easy to handle, about 1 hour. Cut dough into quarters.

Knead 1 portion on floured board until it has an elastic feel. Break into 4 to 6 parts and roll or pat each into a thin 1/4-inch cake.

Slide cakes into heavy skillet half filled with hot oil. Fry until golden brown on both sides. The cake will puff up and get very crisp. Serve hot with butter and syrup.

Makes 24 cakes.

MEXICAN CORN BREAD

1 can (8 ounces) creamed corn

1 can (4 ounces) El Paso green chilies, chopped

1-1/2 cup corn bread or corn muffin mix

3/4 cup Cheddar cheese, grated

Salt and pepper, to taste

1 egg, beaten

2 teaspoons sugar

3/4 cup milk

2 tablespoons vegetable oil

Preheat oven to 325 degrees.

Grease 1-1/2 quart casserole.

Mix all ingredients and pour into casserole. Bake uncovered for 45 minutes to 1 hour. Do not let bread get too brown.

Serves 8 to 10

Note: If you prefer a "hotter" dish, sprinkle chili powder in with the mix. For a milder dish you can substitute chopped green peppers.

CREAM CORN PONES

1 cup unsifted white water-ground corn meal

1/2 teaspoon salt

1/2 cup boiling water

1 tablespoon lard or butter, melted (for corn pones)

1 teaspoon baking powder

1/4 cup thick sweet cream*

1 tablespoon lard or butter, melted (for skillet)

Preheat oven to 450 degrees.

Put corn meal into a bowl. Add salt to corn meal and stir in boiling water. Mixture should resemble dry crumbs. Cover and put in refrigerator for 1 hour.

Combine 1 tablespoon melted lard or butter with baking powder and sweet cream; add to the corn meal mixture. Stir well. The mixture should be a paste, firm enough to handle.

Take heaping tablespoons of the mixture and form into croquette shapes. Melt butter or lard in ovenproof skillet. Put corn pones in skillet; pat tops slightly to flatten. Bake in oven for 30 minutes.

Serve hot with beans or greens.

Makes about 24

*Can also be made with thick sour cream, substituting 1/4 teaspoon baking soda for baking powder.

CALAMONDIN-KUMQUAT MARMALADE

1 cup calamondins

3 cups kumquats

8 cups water

4 cups sugar

Wash, quarter and seed fruit. Chop in processor or by hand. Measure fruit into non-aluminum kettle. Add water and let stand overnight.

Next day, measure 4 cups of mixture into kettle and add 4 cups sugar. Boil rapidly until liquid sheets off spoon. Remove from heat, ladle into hot, sterile jars and seal.

Yields 4 to 6 pints

Note: From "Jams and Jellies Ramble Recipes," Fairchild Tropical Garden

. . . .

CLASSIC CALAMONDIN MARMALADE

Ripe calamondins

Sugar

Measure amount of seeded, chopped calamondins into non-aluminum kettle. Add equal amount of sugar. Boil rapidly to soft jellying point, stirring constantly.

Ladle into hot sterile jars and seal with paraffin.

Note: Pour into a sterilized heavy glass beer mug to within 1 inch of top. Seal with a thin layer of paraffin. Top with cooling paraffin, whipped to a foam. A wonderful gift!

46 Emathla, Seminole leader

PEACOCK'S GUAVA JELLY

The original Peacock family arrived in South Florida from England in
the 1870's. They purchased land at "Jack's Bight," now Coconut Grove
and built the Peacock Inn, the first mainland hotel between Palm
Beach and Key West.

2 pounds ripe guavas, thinly sliced

2-1/4 cups water

1/2 cup lime or lemon juice

7 cups sugar

1 box powdered pectin

Red food coloring (optional)

In a covered pan, simmer guavas 5 minutes in water. Crush with a
masher. Squeeze fruit through cheesecloth and if necessary, add enough
cooking water to make 3-1/2 cups liquid.
In large pan, add lime or lemon juice and sugar to 3-1/2 cups juice.
Bring to a boil, add pectin. Boil 1 minute.
Skim foam from the top of the mixture and add red food coloring if
desired. Pour into sterile jars and cover with wax.

Yields about 2 pints

BEET-RED JELLY

6 medium beets, cleaned, sliced

6 to 7 cups water

1/2 cup lemon juice

2 boxes powered pectin

8 cups sugar

1 box raspberry gelatin

Cover beets with water and cook until juices are released. Remove beets from pan and add lemon juice and pectin to 6 cups of beet juice. Bring to a boil. Add sugar and gelatin and boil 6 minutes.

Ladle into sterile jars and seal.

Makes 3 pints

This recipe brings to mind that wonderful loony species of mankind often found on the beaches, by the Bay, in your spare bedroom, in a hotel or hopelessly lost on our expressways. They worship the sun and the water and seem convinced that "beet-red" is the route to a perfect tan. They record 'most everything with a camera while writing "wish you were here" on post cards which they send off to parts unknown. They dress in lightweight multi-colored clothing regardless of the temperature and often will swim, surf and sunbathe when a "native" wouldn't dream of touching a toe to the Bay.

Yes, they started arriving around the turn of the century and their numbers in our area have increased annually. They come from all directions, in all sizes, speak 'most any language, ask 'most any question and have been known to do 'most anything imaginable or outrageous. That species, near and dear to our hearts and wallets, regardless of unusual behavior, is commonly known as "The Tourist."

CARAMBOLA-GINGER JELLY

4 cups carambola juice

1/4 cup lime juice

7 cups sugar

3 pieces candied ginger, finely chopped

6 ounces liquid pectin

Wash carambolas, cut away outer ribs, quarter and place in large kettle. Do not add water. Simmer 40 minutes, mashing fruit. Strain through cheesecloth.

Combine juices, sugar and ginger in large kettle and bring to a boil. Add pectin, bring back to hard boil for 1 minute. Remove from heat and skim.

Ladle into hot, sterile jars and seal.

Yields about 2 pints

Note: From "Jams and Jellies Ramble Recipes," Fairchild Tropical Garden.

SUMPTUOUS SEAGRAPE JELLY

South Florida seagrapes are usually at their peak in the fall.

4 cups seagrape juice

2 tablespoons lemon juice

5-1/2 cups sugar

1 box powered pectin

Pick fully ripe fruit that have just turned purple. Include a few grapes which are mature but do not show color. Wash. Place in large pot with water to cover and simmer 45 minutes. Strain through cheesecloth.

Combine measured juice and pectin and bring to boil. Add sugar and return to boil. Boil 1 minute. Skim.

Ladle into hot, sterile jars and seal.

Note: From "Tropical Fruit Recipes," Rare Fruit Council of Florida

Bay Buisquine, Harper's New Monthly Magazine, March 1871

SALADS AND SALAD DRESSINGS

The Alamo
Jackson Memorial Hospital
1917

GUAVA SALAD

In 1898, the family of William Burdine opened a tiny frame trading post on South Miami Avenue. Soon they moved to Twelfth Street, now Flagler Street, and the store thrived and expanded in the central business district of the young village. The business remains in that location today.

This recipe was first printed in the *Sunshine Cookbook* by Josephine Jackson, published in 1930, by Burdines Department Store.

| 4 large guavas, peeled, cut into 1/2-inch cubes |
| 2 cups fresh pineapple, diced |
| 1/2 cup lime juice |
| 3 tablespoons sugar |

Toss together, chill and serve on lettuce.

Serves 4 to 6

SUNNY ORANGE-ONION SALAD

| 4 large Florida Navel oranges, peeled, sectioned |
| 1 large purple onion, thinly sliced |
| 1/4 cup Key lime juice |
| 1/3 cup finest quality olive oil |
| Salt and freshly ground black pepper, to taste |
| Pecans or sunflower seeds (optional) |

Separate onion into rings and add to oranges. Toss gently with lime juice, olive oil and seasonings. Marinate in refrigerator at least 1 hour. Arrange on bed of crisp mixed greens. Sprinkle with sunflower seeds or chopped pecans.

Serves 6 to 8

Note: Also good with Poppy Seed Dressing. (See Index.)

Miss Miami hosts Miss America, 1933. (Romer Collection)

TOMATOES PROVENÇAL

4 large tomatoes, halved

Salt and freshly ground pepper, to taste

8 to 12 tablespoons fresh shallots, finely chopped

5 tablespoons basil leaves, finely chopped

5 tablespoons tarragon leaves, finely chopped

5 tablespoons parsley, finely chopped

Marie's French or Blue cheese dressing, to taste

Arrange tomatoes cut side up on serving dish and season generously with salt and pepper.

Sprinkle each tomato half with shallots. Combine herbs and cover tomato halves with a thick green layer. Top with dressing.

Serves 8

INSALATA DI RADICCHIO E ARUGULA

This tart salad has a very different taste. It is excellent served after the entrée to cleanse the palate.

2 small heads radicchio

2 bunches arugula

2 stalks fresh endive

Wash, drain and dry radicchio, arugula and endive. Wrap in towel and chill.

Tear radicchio into bite-size pieces. Chop arugula. Slice endive into 1/4-inch rounds. Toss with Vinaigrette Dressing. (See Index.) Season to taste.

Serves 6 to 8

Note: These salad greens are available in most gourmet produce stores.

CUBED CUCUMBER AND TOMATO IN YOGURT

Serve in small individual bowls with curries or other spicy dishes.

1 medium cucumber, peeled, seeded, in 1/2-inch cubes

1 tablespoon onion, finely chopped

1 teaspoon salt

1 small ripe tomato, peeled, in 1/2-inch cubes

1 tablespoon fresh cilantro, chopped

1 cup plain yogurt

1 teaspoon ground cumin, toasted

Combine cucumber, onion and salt in a small bowl. Let mixture rest 5 minutes. Drain to remove excess liquid. Add tomato and cilantro; mix thoroughly.

Combine yogurt and cumin. Pour over vegetables, turning them to coat evenly. Season to taste, cover tightly and refrigerate for at least 1 hour.

Serves 2

TOMATOES AND MOZZARELLA VINAIGRETTE

2 large beefsteak tomatoes

1 pound Bufala Mozzarella cheese, thinly sliced*

5 to 6 fresh basil leaves, chopped

Arrange on platter, alternating with slices of tomatoes and cheese. Sprinkle with basil.

VINAIGRETTE DRESSING

1/4 cup tarragon vinegar

3/4 cup finest quality olive oil

1 teaspoon dry mustard

2 cloves garlic, chopped extra fine

Salt and pepper, to taste

Whisk ingredients together. Pour over tomatoes and cheese.

Serve 4 to 6

*Bufala or Bufalina Mozzarella is a delicious, but very perishable cheese made from the milk of Italian water buffalos. It is available only in the best gourmet cheese shops.

HOT AND TANGY TOMATO ASPIC

1 package (3 ounces) orange-flavored gelatin
1-1/4 cups hot water
1 can (8 ounces) tomato sauce with green peppers
1-1/2 tablespoons vinegar
1/2 teaspoon garlic salt
Dash of pepper, onion juice, horseradish and cayenne pepper
Worcestershire sauce, to taste

Dissolve gelatin in hot water. Add tomato sauce, vinegar, garlic salt, pepper and Worcestershire sauce. Blend well. Pour into individual molds and chill.

Serves 4 to 6

Note: This recipe can easily be doubled. Use a ring mold and fill the center with cottage cheese.

FLORIDA PALM SALAD

This recipe was one of Bessie Gibbs' most famous. She owned the Old Island Hotel on Cedar Key. The peanut butter dressing makes it outstanding.

4 cups palm hearts (swamp cabbage may be substituted)
1 cup pineapple, cubed
1/4 cup dates, chopped
1/4 cup candied or preserved ginger, chopped

Toss ingredients lightly.

PEANUT BUTTER DRESSING

4 tablespoons vanilla ice cream
2 tablespoons mayonnaise
2 tablespoons crunchy peanut butter
Pineapple juice or preserved ginger juice
Drop of green food coloring

Mix ice cream, mayonnaise and peanut butter thoroughly. Thin with either pineapple or ginger juice, pour over salad and serve.

Serves 8 to 10

VEGETABLE SALAD WITH TOMATO-BASIL DRESSING

3/4 cup celery

3/4 cup carrots, peeled

3/4 cup green peppers, seeded

3/4 cup small onions, peeled

3/4 cup cored tomatoes, cubed

3/4 cup small yellow squash

3/4 cup small cucumbers

Thinly slice vegetables and layer into a 2-quart glass bowl. Other vegetables such as radishes, parsnips, red peppers or zucchini may be
substituted.

TOMATO-BASIL DRESSING

1/2 teaspoon garlic, finely minced

1/4 cup tomato sauce

1/3 cup red wine vinegar

1 tablespoon sugar

1-1/2 teaspoons basil

1 teaspoon Worcestershire sauce

1/4 teaspoon dry mustard

1/4 teaspoon Tabasco sauce

1 cup vegetable oil

Salt and freshly ground pepper, to taste

Blend all ingredients except oil. Slowly add oil in thin stream while
whisking. Pour over the vegetables, cover and refrigerate several hours
or overnight.

Serves 6 to 10

CHRISTMAS SALAD

This salad is especially pretty for a buffet during the Christmas holidays because of the red and green colors.

1 package (7 ounces) frozen Chinese pea pods, thawed

1/2 pound fresh mushrooms, washed, thinly sliced

1 sweet red pepper, seeded, cut into 1/4-inch strips

Layer pea pods, mushrooms and red pepper slices in a medium salad bowl. (A glass bowl shows off the salad best.) When ready to serve, pour dressing over the salad and toss until the vegetables are well coated.

DRESSING

1/3 cup salad oil

2 tablespoons white wine vinegar

1 tablespoon lemon juice

1 clove garlic, crushed

1 tablespoon sugar

1/2 teaspoon salt

Combine all ingredients.

Serves 6

1 926 DURING "THE BOOM"

Yuletide is a cheery season
Giving me a darn good reason,
To send my Christmas wishes hearty.
And invite you to my usual party.

On New Year's afternoon at four,
Enter the Roney Plaza door.
Bring dancing eyes and dancing legs,
Be a good egg with the other eggs,

Warm your heart with frothy nogs,
Warm your lips 'neath mistletoe logs
So come and raise ye merry ned
With that old skate, your Uncle Ed.
        R.S.V.P. E.R. Thomas
        "Seaweed"
        Miami Beach

1929 AFTER "THE CRASH"

Please accept these hearty wishes
From a poor but honest friend
For ye gods and little fishes,
These are all that I can send.

These awful storms! Those awful stocks!
What they've done to you and me!
Nothin' in our Christmas socks!
Nothin' on our Christmas tree!

So how about a dance or two
With Uncle Ed on New Year's Day
How about a few nogs too,
To drive the darned old blues away?

How about R.S.V.P.
Saying that you won't be late?
The music stops at six you see
Your Uncle Ed, the same Old Skate.
        E.R. Thomas
        "Seaweed"
        Roney Plaza
        Three to Six
        Miami Beach

TORTELLINI SALAD WITH DIJON VINAIGRETTE

2 pounds tortellini

1 pound broccoli, cut into bite-size florets

1 head cauliflower, cut into florets

1 pound green beans

1 pound mushroom caps, quartered

2 cans artichoke hearts, halved

1/2 pound red onions, thinly sliced

1 bunch scallions, chopped

1 green bell pepper, cut to julienne

1 red bell pepper, cut to julienne

3 carrots, thinly sliced

3 medium yellow squash, thinly sliced

3 medium zucchini, thinly sliced

1 can black olives

1 pint cherry tomatoes

The day before serving, blanch broccoli and cauliflower for 2 minutes. Blanch green beans for 5 minutes.

Combine all vegetables with Dijon Vinaigrette Salad Dressing. Chill overnight, tossing often.

Before serving prepare tortellini according to package directions and set aside to cool. Drain vegetables and add tortellini.

DIJON VINAIGRETTE SALAD DRESSING

2 tablespoons Dijon-style mustard

3/4 cup salad oil

1/4 cup wine vinegar

1/2 teaspoon salt

1/4 teaspoon pepper

Blend all ingredients thoroughly. Makes 1 cup.

Serves 20

ZIPPY BEEF SALAD WITH DIJON DRESSING

1/4 cup capers

2 cups small new potatoes, boiled and sliced

1 cup scallions, finely sliced

2 cups celery with tops, chopped

3 cups lean roast beef, sliced, cut into 1-1/2 inch squares

8 sour pickles, sliced

1 cup cherry tomatoes

Greens, such as Boston or curly leaf lettuce

Combine first 7 ingredients and toss in a large bowl. Arrange them on the salad greens and serve with Dijon Dressing.

DIJON DRESSING

6 eggs, hard cooked

3 tablespoons Dijon-style mustard

1 cup olive oil

1 clove garlic rubbed into 1-1/2 teaspoons salt; discard garlic

1 teaspoon black pepper, finely ground

1/3 cup vinegar

Dash of Tabasco, or to taste

Sliced pickled walnuts*

Mash 3 egg yolks (reserve and chop whites for garnish). Mix in mustard, oil, salt, pepper, vinegar and Tabasco. Pour dressing over beef salad.

Garnish with 3 eggs, quartered, sliced walnuts and chopped egg whites. Trim plate with lettuce.

Serves 8

*Available in all gourmet shops.

"The tender lettuce brings on softer sleep."

"Pineapple aids digestion, and will, it is said, sweeten the voice; oranges, grapefruit and lemons will clear the complexion."

"Salads should never be sour, but so delicately blended that no seasoning predominates. Distrust the condiment that bites too soon."

– Florida Salads, A Collection of Dainty, Wholesome Salad Recipes that will appeal to the most fastidious. *Francis Barber Harris*, 1922, Jacksonville, Florida

Miami Courthouse

GARDEN WILD RICE SALAD

1 package (6 ounces) long grain wild rice

1/4 pound small white fresh mushroom caps sautéed

1 can artichokes, drained, trimmed and chopped

3/4 cup Italian dressing

1/2 cup frozen green peas, thawed and drained (garnish)

6 cherry tomatoes, halved (garnish)

Parsley (garnish)

Cook rice according to package directions; add mushrooms and artichokes.

Combine onions with sufficient Italian dressing to moisten. Add to rice and let marinate in refrigerator overnight.

Remove from refrigerator an hour before serving, toss well.

Garnish with green peas, tomatoes and parsley.

Serves 4 to 6

BACON, SPINACH AND RICE SALAD

4 cups rice, cooked

1/2 cup Italian dressing

1 tablespoon soy sauce

1/2 teaspoon sugar

1/2 cup scallions with green tops, chopped

1/2 cup celery, chopped

2 cups fresh raw spinach, shredded

5 to 6 slices cooked bacon, crumbled

Mix Italian dressing, soy sauce and sugar. Toss with the rice and chill.

At serving time add the remaining ingredients.

Serves 4 to 6

ORIENTAL CHICKEN SALAD

1/2 cup ham, cut to julienne

3 cups cooked chicken, shredded

1/4 cup sesame seeds, toasted

4 ribs celery, thinly sliced

1 cucumber, peeled, thinly sliced

5 scallions, sliced

1/2 head iceberg lettuce, shredded

1 handful agar-agar, soaked, drained*

1 raw egg

1 tablespoon water

Toss first 9 ingredients in a salad bowl.

Beat the egg with water; pour into non-stick skillet over medium heat. Tilt pan to cover bottom evenly. When set, not browned, remove from pan. Roll; cool, slice thinly. Add to salad.

Toss salad with dressing.

DRESSING

1 clove garlic, crushed

1/3 cup sesame seed oil, warmed

Salt and pepper, to taste

1 tablespoon soy sauce

1/4 teaspoon sugar

1/4 cup cider vinegar

Mix all ingredients thoroughly.

Serves 6

*Agar-Agar is a dried seaweed available in Chinese or specialty stores.

THE CORAL ROCK KEYS
The Florida Keys, first called "The Martyrs" by the Span-ish because of the twisted shapes of the trees, are a series of coral rock islands extending south and west from the tip of the mainland.

Over thousands of years the living coral was compressed and changed to coral rock, a beautiful soft limestone showing the whorls and patterns of the original skeletal shapes. Windley Key, south of Key Largo at mile marker 84, has old quarries which were carved from the Keys' highest hill, 16 feet above sea level. Much of the foundation stone for Flagler's overseas railroad was cut from that hill. The intricately patterned rock, often called Keystone, was used as facing for some of Miami's great buildings, including the old downtown post office.

What remains in those rock faces are the curving signatures of marine life fos-silized for perhaps 100,000 years. This 32-acre quarry contains the world's only petrified coral reef.

ROYAL PALM CHICKEN SALAD

3 cups chicken, cooked and diced

1 pound shrimp, cooked and cleaned

8 ounces pineapple chunks

4 fresh ripe peaches, cubed

1 pound pasta twists, cooked

1/2 cup celery, finely diced

1/4 cup onions, minced

Fresh fruit (garnish)

Combine all ingredients in a large bowl. Add dressing and marinate in refrigerator overnight.

Garnish with fresh fruit.

DRESSING

1 cup light corn oil

1 cup lemon juice, freshly squeezed

1/2 cup Dijon-style mustard

1 can (14 ounces) sweetened condensed milk

Mix dressing ingredients in bowl, whisk together until frothy white.

Serves 8 to 10

CHICKEN SALAD MANDALAY

2/3 cup raisins

1/2 cup white wine

3 cups chicken, cooked, cut into bite-size pieces

2/3 cup coconut, shredded

2/3 cup dry-roasted peanuts, unsalted

1-1/2 cups Hellmann's mayonnaise

1/2 cup chutney

1 avocado

1 banana

Soak raisins in wine for about 1 hour. Drain and combine with chicken, coconut, peanuts, mayonnaise and chutney. Chill thoroughly.

At serving time peel and dice avocado and slice banana. Add to salad mixture. Serve on crisp greens.

Serves 6

Royal Palm Hotel built in 1898

ENU GRAND OPENING – ROYAL PALM HOTEL
January 17, 1897

Green Turtle Soup
Escalop du Pompano, à la Normandie
Filet du Boeuf à la Cavaur
Sweetbread Glacée with Asparagus Tips
Quail sur Canapés
Ribs of Beef
Claret Jelly
Tutti-frutti Ice Cream

THE FLORIDA CRAWFISH *South Florida settlers developed their own food vocabulary. For example "sours" were limes, "dillies" were sapodillas, "pawpaws" were papayas, and rock, spiny or Florida lobster are still called "crawfish."*

Hardy pioneers didn't worry much about the difference between the big clawed giant lobster found in New England and Europe and the miniature fresh-water delicacy so treasured around the world, especially in New Orleans. Early Miamians knew only that they liked what they caught and it was plentiful.

When you first handle a fresh caught crawfish, remember that the shell is sharp and that puncture wounds will be slow to heal. Chill your catch in ice immediately for at least one hour. If not well chilled, the meat will stick to the shell when cooked. There is very little meat in the feelers and it is unnecessary to cook anything but the tail. If you remove the meat from the shell, wash it carefully before cooking to keep the edges from darkening.

Never, ever, overcook them. Usually no more than 10 to 15 minutes are needed to poach or broil Florida lobster, depending on the thickness of the tail.

FLORIDA LOBSTER SALAD

The clawless Florida lobster is locally referred to as "crawfish."

6 Florida lobsters, about 1 pound each
2 avocados, sliced
Lemon juice
Lettuce leaves

Immerse lobsters, head first, into salted, boiling water. Allow water to return to a boil and continue cooking until lobster turns red. Remove from heat and plunge into cold water to stop the cooking process; drain.

Split each lobster in half lengthwise with a sharp knife. Remove sand vein. Most of the meat is in the tail, but some can also be found in larger segments of the legs. Remove meat and cut into bite-size pieces.

Arrange avocados brushed with lemon juice on lettuce leaves and chill.

DRESSING

1 cup celery, chopped
Key lime juice, to taste
Hellmann's mayonnaise, to taste
1 tablespoon capers
Paprika (garnish)

Mix all ingredients except paprika and toss with lobster chunks. Serve over avocado slices. Sprinkle with paprika.

Serves 6

Note: If frozen lobster tails are used, allow to cook an additional 2 to 3 minutes after they turn red.

KEY LARGO SHRIMP SALAD

2 pounds large shrimp, cooked, peeled, deveined; halved or quartered

1 teaspoon red pepper, seeded, chopped

1 teaspoon green pepper, seeded, chopped

1 cup celery, diced

2 hard cooked eggs, chopped

1/4 cup mayonnaise

Salt and pepper, to taste

1 tablespoon fresh Key lime juice

1 tablespoon small capers

1 teaspoon fresh dill or 1/2 teaspoon dried dill

Toss all ingredients together and chill for at least 1 hour.

Serves 4 to 6

Nice catch! Key Largo Anglers Club, 1932. (Romer Collection)

KEY LARGO
Key Largo, the northernmost of the Florida Keys, is an accessible weekend getaway for many Miami residents as well as a sunning and fishing paradise for tourists. Perhaps its greatest claim to fame is the 1948 movie Key Largo, directed by John Huston. Considered one of Humphrey Bogart's classics, it also starred Edward G. Robinson, Lionel Barrymore, Lauren Bacall, and Claire Trevor portraying a group trapped by a kingpin gangster in an isolated Florida Keys hotel. Those great actors breathed life into the film which, though it may have lacked a certain substance and coherence and contained such incongruities as a thirty minute hurricane, has sustained its reputation as entertaining drama.

That "isolated hotel," on the overseas highway, has changed ownership through the years and presently is known as The Caribbean Club. There is a large sign proclaiming it as the place where Key Largo was filmed.

CRAB MEAT AND LYCHEE NUT SALAD

1 avocado, cut in half

Juice of 1 lime

6 to 8 ounces crab meat

1/2 cup lychee nuts, peeled

2 tablespoons celery, finely chopped

Sprinkle avocado with lime juice and place on lettuce leaves. In a bowl, toss crab meat, lychees and celery very lightly. Fill avocado halves and top with your favorite fruit salad dressing.

Serves 2

. . . .

GORGONZOLA DRESSING

This is a marvelous dressing served chilled over crisp romaine lettuce and Belgian endive. The crunchy nut garnish adds interest to a rich combination of flavors.

1/2 cup Parmesan cheese, grated

5 ounces Gorgonzola cheese, crumbled

1/4 cup tarragon or wine vinegar

1/2 cup finest quality olive oil

Dash cayenne pepper

1 teaspoon fines herbs

1/2 cup walnuts, coarsely chopped (garnish)

Cream all ingredients except nuts in blender or food processor for 2 minutes. Chill briefly before serving.

Serves 8

SAGA BLUE SALAD DRESSING

8 ounces sour cream

1/2 cup Saga Blue cheese, crumbled

1/2 cup Hellmann's mayonnaise

2 tablespoons lemon juice

1/4 teaspoon salt (optional)

1/8 teaspoon pepper (optional)

1/2 teaspoon Worcestershire sauce

Mix all ingredients. Best if made a few hours in advance.

Makes about 2 cups

. . . .

CLARA'S POPPY SEED DRESSING

This pioneer recipe was in the collection of the mother of local historian and author Dr. Thelma Peters.

1-1/2 cups sugar

2 tablespoons dry mustard

2 tablespoons salt

3 tablespoons onions, grated

2/3 cup white vinegar

2 cups vegetable oil

3 tablespoons poppy seeds

Mix all ingredients except oil and poppy seeds until sugar is dissolved. Beat rapidly while adding oil slowly. Add poppy seeds and refrigerate.

Makes about 3 cups

FISH AND SHELLFISH

For years, the treacherous Florida reefs provided a livelihood for salvagers, many of them from the Bahamas, who swooped in on grounded vessels, stripped them of cargo and valuables and returned home to sell the plunder. In order to regulate salvage operations, the United States government established Key West as an official port of entry and required all wreckers to register any salvage taken from United States waters. Immediately, Key West became a thriving city with buyers, sellers, entrepreneurs and all the other trappings of a lively business center. At one time in the 1830's, Key West had the highest per capita income in the country.

Anyone or anything destined for Miami arrived via Key West, first sailing there and then taking a smaller vessel back to Miami. Many felt Key West's importance as the deepest seaport south of Norfolk, Virginia and it's proximity to the Panama Canal were the real reasons Henry Flagler extended his railroad south. He once said he doubted Miami would ever become more than a little fishing village for his hotel guests.

Time has dramatically changed the positions of these two cities. Today Key West is a colorful resort and fishing village, where tourists and residents alike gather on Mallory Pier to applaud the sunset, while Miami is the major international city.

KEY WEST SHRIMP

5 pounds shrimp in shell

1 cup Italian dressing

Juice of 4 Key limes

2 cups (4 sticks) butter

4 tablespoons pepper, freshly ground

Preheat oven to 450 degrees.

Place shrimp in baking dish. Cover with salad dressing and Key lime juice. Dot with butter and cover with pepper. Bake 10 to 15 minutes. Dip French bread in the sauce, it's delicious.

Serves 6

Gingerbread architecture, Key West

SHRIMP IN SZECHWAN GARLIC SAUCE

1-1/2 pounds raw shrimp, peeled and deveined

1 tablespoon cornstarch

1 teaspoon white wine

1 egg white, beaten

1-1/2 teaspoons sesame oil

1 tablespoon fresh ginger, chopped

2 tablespoons green onions, chopped

2 tablespoons water chestnuts, chopped

2 tablespoons black fungus,* soaked and chopped

1 teaspoon fresh garlic, minced

1 tablespoon hot bean paste or hoisin sauce

2 tablespoons soy sauce

1/2 teaspoon vinegar

1 teaspoon sugar

1/4 cup chicken stock

2 teaspoons cornstarch

2 teaspoons water

Dissolve 1 tablespoon cornstarch in wine, add beaten egg white and shrimp, mixing to coat well. Marinate at least 30 minutes.

Heat a wok until it is very hot. Add oil and ginger, stir-fry shrimp quickly until pink. Remove shrimp. Add green onions, water chestnuts, fungus, garlic and hot bean paste; stir-fry a few seconds to blend ingredients. Add soy sauce, vinegar, sugar and chicken stock and bring to a boil. Mix 2 teaspoons cornstarch with water and add to wok with shrimp. Mix until sauce becomes translucent.

Serves 6

*Called "Clouds Ears," they are available in Oriental food markets or occasionally in your supermarket.

COLD SHRIMP CURRY WITH WHITE GRAPES

1-1/4 pounds shrimp, cooked, peeled, deveined and chilled

1 to 2 tablespoons curry powder, to taste

1 cup mayonnaise

Dash of cayenne pepper

Sprinkling of white pepper, freshly ground

3/4 cup seedless white grapes

Bunch of watercress

1/2 cup almonds, slivered and blanched

Mango chutney

Thoroughly mix curry powder, mayonnaise, cayenne and white pepper in a bowl. Add grapes and lightly toss together. Pour mixture over shrimp. Refrigerate, covered, for 1 hour.

Toss lightly, serve on a bed of watercress. Sprinkle with almonds.

Serve with mango chutney.

Serves 3 to 4

SHRIMP NEWBURG WITH MUSHROOMS

2 pounds of shrimp, cooked, peeled and deveined

4 tablespoons (1/2 stick) butter

4 tablespoons flour

2 cups cream or half-and-half

6 tablespoons tomato sauce

1/2 teaspoon salt

1-1/2 tablespoons Worcestershire sauce

1 pound fresh mushrooms, lightly sautéed

1/4 teaspoon paprika

1/8 teaspoon cayenne pepper

1/2 cup dry sherry

Melt butter. Blend flour into butter and add cream or half-and-half. Stir until sauce thickens. Add tomato sauce, salt, Worcestershire sauce, shrimp, mushrooms, cayenne pepper, paprika and sherry. Heat to boiling point and immediately remove from stove.

Serve over hot rice.

Serves 4 to 6

SILVER BLUFF SHRIMP AND PASTA

Miami's Bay Shore Drive is distinguished by a high gray ridge of limestone called the Silver Bluff. This is one of the few visible remnants of the rim of the historic Everglades basin.

2 pounds raw shrimp, (18 to 24 per pound) peeled and deveined

1/2 cup (1 stick) butter

1/4 cup olive oil

1 pound fresh mushrooms, sliced

Salt and pepper, to taste

1/4 teaspoon Italian herbs

1 cup chicken broth

1 cup dry white wine

1 pound fresh pasta, cooked

Romano cheese, grated (garnish)

Parsley, chopped (garnish)

Melt butter over medium heat and add olive oil. Sauté mushrooms and shrimp until shrimp turns pink. Season with salt, pepper and Italian herbs.

Add chicken broth and dry white wine. Simmer for 1 minute to blend flavors. Taste to correct seasonings.

Pour over fresh pasta, cooked until tender but still firm. Sprinkle generously with Romano cheese and chopped parsley.

Serves 6 to 8

SHRIMP BRINJAL

This recipe was the 1981 March of Dimes Gourmet Gala winner.

16 large raw shrimp, peeled and deveined

2 tablespoons onion, chopped

2 ounces vegetable oil

2 cloves garlic, minced

2 chili peppers, finely chopped

2 tablespoons curry powder

1 to 2 tablespoons tomato paste

1 cup water

2 medium eggplants, peeled and diced into 3/4-inch cubes

Salt, to taste

Lemon juice, freshly squeezed (to taste)

1 tablespoon fresh coconut cream*

Over medium heat, sauté onion in oil until soft. Add next 6 ingredients and cook until eggplant is almost tender.

Add shrimp, salt and lemon juice and cook 3 minutes more. At serving time stir in coconut cream.

Serves 4

Note: For a wonderful accompaniment, serve cucumbers in plain yogurt and poppadums, a lightly fried paper-thin bread available in Indian markets.

*Remove meat from a fresh coconut, grate and wrap in cheesecloth; pour boiling water over cheesecloth catching liquid in a bowl. Place liquid in refrigerator and chill. Cream will rise to the top.

ISLANDS FOR SALE

It has been said that during the height of the post-war real estate boom, Carl Fisher, the ingenious and energetic developer of Miami Beach, would row a customer out in Biscayne Bay, have him pick out a smooth spot of water and offer him an island. Fisher created Star Island in 1917 completely by dredging and it was so successful that other man-made islands soon dotted the Bay until there were 26 in all. The last one, Pelican Island, named for the birds that perch on each of the pilings outlining the island, still lies under four feet of water, unchanged since 1926 because of various disputes and bankruptcies.

Many of the homes on those islands have belonged to a number of notable and wealthy personalities such as R.J. Reynolds, J.C. Penney and Elliott Roosevelt. Even today, pointing them out is a popular feature of boat tours on Biscayne Bay. A guide's spiel is little changed over the years: "... There are four ways to become a millionaire: work for it, marry it, inherit it or steal it. All four kinds have lived here."

They always point out the home owned by the notorious gangster Al Capone who, after serving a ten-month prison term, set up housekeeping in the former Anheuser-Busch mansion on Star Island.

STAR ISLAND SHRIMP PILAU

1 pound raw shrimp, peeled and deveined

1 green pepper, seeded and chopped

1 large onion, chopped

1 cup celery, chopped

1/3 cup vegetable oil

8 ounces chili sauce

1 tablespoon flour

1 tablespoon butter

1 small can button mushrooms, drain and reserve liquid

Dash Worcestershire sauce

Dash Tabasco sauce

Paprika, to taste

Sauté pepper, onion and celery in oil until tender. Add chili sauce.

Mix flour, butter and liquid from mushrooms to make a sauce. Add sauce and mushrooms to sautéed vegetables. Cook 40 minutes. Add Worcestershire sauce, Tabasco sauce, paprika and shrimp. Cook 5 minutes and serve over rice.

Serves 2 to 3

SCAMPI VOUVRAY

1-1/4 pounds raw shrimp, peeled and deveined

3 tablespoons butter

3 tablespoons Vouvray white wine

1 or 2 cloves garlic, finely minced

Salt and pepper, to taste

Melt butter and add wine and garlic. Place shrimp on broiler pan. Pour sauce over shrimp and season with salt and pepper. Broil 3 inches from flame for 5 minutes turning once. Serve over rice.

Serves 4

• •

OLD-FASHIONED OYSTER FRITTERS

Miami's first newspaper, *The Miami Metropolis,* was founded in 1896. This recipe is a reprint from the November 16, 1909 edition.

"Beat 2 eggs lightly and stir into them a cup of milk and a pound of flour that has been sifted with a teaspoonful of baking powder. If batter is too stiff add more milk. Stir 25 chopped oysters into the batter, beat hard and drop by the spoonful into deep boiling fat. As soon as brown, drain in a hot colander. Transfer to a hot dish and serve."

Serves 3 to 4

MUSSELS IN WINE SAUCE

3 dozen mussels, scrubbed and de-bearded

1 cup dry white wine

1 cup heavy cream

1 medium onion, finely chopped

1/4 cup parsley, finely chopped

2 tablespoons butter

1/2 teaspoon salt

1/4 teaspoon cayenne pepper

Discard any mussels that are not tightly closed. Scrub well under cold running water to remove sand, seaweed and barnacles. A stiff brush or steel wool works very nicely.

Place mussels in a large bowl and cover with cold water. Let stand 1 to 2 hours.

Drain mussels, put in a large kettle with the wine, cream, onion, parsley, butter, salt and pepper. Cover tightly and bring to a boil. Continue cooking for 3 minutes or until shells open.

Place mussels in large flat soup bowls and cover with broth. Serve with French bread.

Serves 4

CONCH FRITTERS WITH PINEAPPLE PICANTE SAUCE

2 pounds conch, ground or finely chopped

4 green peppers, seeded and chopped

4 onions, chopped

3 cups all-purpose flour

2 tablespoons baking powder

2 eggs

1-1/3 cups milk

Salt and pepper, freshly ground (to taste)

Vegetable oil

Combine conch, green peppers and onions in a large bowl. Add flour and baking powder. Stir well.

Break eggs into bowl, beat with fork and stir into mixture. Add up to 1-1/3 cups milk and seasonings. Blend until mixture has absorbed all the flour and forms a very sticky dough.

Heat 1/2-inch of oil in a heavy skillet. Drop batter from a tablespoon into the oil and flatten with a spatula. Cook on each side until deep golden brown. Keep warm in the oven until all the fritters have been cooked.

Serve with lime wedges and Pineapple Picante Sauce.

PINEAPPLE PICANTE SAUCE

1 cup catsup	1-1/2 teaspoons garlic salt
1/4 teaspoon cayenne pepper	1 tablespoon dill weed

3 tablespoons Worcestershire sauce

3 tablespoons spicy prepared mustard

1 can (20 ounces) crushed unsweetened pineapple, drained

Place all ingredients in a food processor and pulse several times to mix thoroughly. If you prefer a chunky sauce, mix by hand.

Serves 8

Note: To serve as appetizers reduce size of fritters.

BAHAMA CRACKED CONCH

1 to 1-1/2 pounds conch, tenderized*

2 eggs, separated

3/4 cup beer, room temperature

1 tablespoon oil

1 cup flour, sifted

1 tablespoon soy sauce

1/2 teaspoon turmeric

Flour for dredging

Oil for frying

Separate eggs and set whites aside. Combine egg yolks, beer, oil, flour, soy sauce and turmeric. Blend until smooth. Beat egg whites until stiff and fold into the batter.

Cut conch into 8 or more pieces. Dip into flour, then into batter. Fry in an uncrowded pan until golden. A very crisp crust will form. Drain on paper towels.

Serve very hot with lime wedges and Pickapeppa sauce which is available in grocery stores.

Serves 4

*When buying conch, ask to have it run through the tenderizer machine twice.

OLD CONCHS NEVER DIE – THEY JUST "CONK OUT"

Conchs are people, too – real natives of the Florida Keys who take great pride in their nickname. They are descendants of British and Bahamian seafarers and early settlers from young America's southern states. It is possible, but seldom discussed, that a few northerners were among the first to arrive.

No one can earn the right to be called a Conch. You must be born one. Even today, newcomers to the Keys are called "strangers."

Authentic Conchs are bound to have some sea water in their veins. Their forebears arrived by sea, the one-and-only pioneer highway. They live surrounded by the sea, breathing the rich, salt-laden air. Most old homes still have cisterns for saving the abundant rain water. The soil, such as it is, is a crust of limestone where dynamite serves better than a plow, and seaweed was the first fertilizer.

It's remarkable that so many of the seeds planted by man or deposited by birds, wind and sea flourish there. Bougainvillea and a wonderful variety of flowering plants thrive in the Keys, more colorful than on the mainland.

Conch families also thrived there and developed their own traditions. In the old days, a conch shell mounted on a pole in the yard would announce that a new "conch" baby had been born. Passing sailors would signal the news to other residents on a wonderfully resonant conch shell horn.

"A GRAND ENTRANCE"
La Puerta del Sol, or The Gate of the Sun, was another name for The Douglas Entrance to Coral Gables. Of all the elegant portals, this was the grandest.

More than one million dollars was spent to build the entrance as a reception center for prospective Gables land buyers.

Construction began in 1924 on the first phase of the building: the library, ballroom, apartments, offices and the soaring archway. Although there were plans for an entire Mediterranean village, only about one-third of the proposed structure was ever built. For example: there was an elevator shaft, but they couldn't afford an elevator; people who wanted to go to the top floor ballroom walked two flights on a very narrow circular staircase.

Even though the first tenants moved into the building in 1927, it remained unpainted for several years because the architect and his assistant couldn't agree on a color.

After the Boom years, the property went through a number of neglectful hands and redevelopment plans were dropped for financial reasons. In 1964 the owners wanted to raze the beautiful structure to build a supermarket! However, it remains a fabulous Coral Gables landmark because of the efforts of the Villagers and other alert preservationists.

DOUGLAS ENTRANCE DEVILED CRAB

The Villagers, organized in 1966, selected the Douglas Entrance, which was slated for destruction, for its first preservation and restoration project.

1 pound crab meat, fresh or canned, flaked

2 stalks celery, finely chopped

2 medium onions, finely chopped

1 bell pepper, finely chopped

2 tablespoons butter

15 saltine crackers, crumbled

2 eggs, beaten

2 to 3 tablespoons milk

2 tablespoons mayonnaise

Salt and pepper, to taste

Dash of Tabasco sauce

1 teaspoon Worcestershire sauce

1 cup buttered bread crumbs

Preheat oven to 350 degrees.

Sauté celery, onions and pepper in butter. Mix all ingredients except bread crumbs. Put in individual serving dishes or single casserole and cover with bread crumbs. Bake for 30 minutes.

Serves 4

CORAL GABLES CRAB CAKES

1 pound crab meat, fresh or canned

1-1/2 tablespoons saltine cracker crumbs

1-1/2 tablespoons flour

1 egg

1 teaspoon Old Bay seafood seasoning

2 tablespoons mayonnaise

Oil and butter

Toss together the crab meat, cracker crumbs and flour. Beat egg in bowl with Old Bay seasoning and mayonnaise. Mix lightly with crab meat. Form into patties and sauté in mixture of oil and butter until golden.

Serves 2 to 4

The Biltmore Hotel, Coral Gables landmark

ERRICK'S "CITY BEAUTIFUL"

George Merrick was the Master Planner of Coral Gables, "The City Beautiful." He had the same comprehensive vision of his city that Carl Fisher did of Miami Beach. While the ground was still raw, both men could see affluent homes, tall shade trees, schools and churches and swimming pools.

Merrick's city would feature dramatic Spanish-Mediterranean architecture, elegant boulevards with fountains, reflecting pools, waterways and canals. Beautiful city gateways would greet the visitors.

When he heard complaints that his lots were too far inland, he bought more land and extended the Coral Gables Waterway to Biscayne Bay, thus creating more waterfront property. When buyers were reluctant to come, he sent gaily painted buses to get them. He saw to it that there were entertainers, dignitaries and huge crowds for the ground breaking and grand opening celebrations of his major edifices: City Hall, Douglas Entrance, Venetian Pool and the Miami Biltmore Hotel.

By 1925 Merrick had turned his expanded family plantation into the single largest real estate venture in the country. It has been said that he made 150 million dollars in sales ... and lost the same amount when the bubble burst following the 1926 hurricane. The city he founded lives on, maturing gracefully, fulfilling his dreams.

LOBSTER THERMIDOR Á LA BILTMORE

3 lobsters, split	3 tablespoons flour
3/4 cup (1-1/2 sticks) butter	1-1/2 cups milk
1-1/2 cups mushrooms, sliced	1/2 cup dry sherry
3/4 cup scallions, chopped	1/4 teaspoon salt
3 egg yolks (save whites for topping)	Dash white pepper
Tabasco sauce, to taste	Dash nutmeg
5 tablespoons Italian cheese, grated	
1-1/2 tablespoons shallots or onions, finely chopped	

Carefully remove lobster meat from shells and set aside.

In a large skillet melt butter and sauté mushrooms, scallions and shallots until soft, not browned. Remove with slotted spoon and set aside.

Place lobster meat in skillet and sauté until firm and pink. Remove cooked lobster and cut into bite-size pieces. Set aside.

Add flour to the skillet, stirring well to prevent lumps. Add milk and sherry and cook until thick and bubbly.

Beat egg yolks; slowly add 1/2 cup of the warm sauce to the beaten yolks (this prevents curdling). Pour the sauce mixture back into pan, adding lobster pieces, scallions, shallots, mushrooms, salt, cheese, pepper, nutmeg and Tabasco. Keep mixture warm while making soufflé topping.

TOPPING

3 egg whites
1-1/2 cups mayonnaise
3 tablespoons Italian cheese, grated
1 tablespoon lemon juice
Paprika, to taste

Beat egg whites until stiff but not dry. Fold in mayonnaise, cheese and lemon juice. Place lobster mixture in 8 ramekins. Spread soufflé topping over each to cover. Sprinkle with paprika. Place under the broiler until top is brown and bubbly. Serve immediately with lemon wedges.

Serves 8

LUSCIOUS LIGHTHOUSE LOBSTER

1 cup green onions, chopped	1 cup chicken stock
1 cup fresh mushrooms, sliced	1 cup dry white wine
1 cup currants, plumped, drained	3 tablespoons flour
1/2 cup celery, chopped	1 cup milk
2 egg yolks, beaten	
1 teaspoon lemon juice	
Salt and white pepper, to taste	
2 pounds raw Florida lobster, shelled and deveined	
1/2 cup (1 stick) butter, divided in half	
1 cup raw shrimp, peeled, deveined and diced	
1/4 cup Mozzarella cheese, shredded	
1-1/2 cups heavy cream	
Bread crumbs for topping	
Watercress (garnish)	

Preheat oven to 350 degrees.

Melt half the butter in a large, heavy saucepan. Cut lobster into 1/2-inch pieces. Sauté the lobster, onions, mushrooms, currants and celery until the lobster turns pink and the vegetables are tender. Add the chicken stock and wine and simmer for 1 minute, stirring well. Remove from heat and set aside.

In another pan, melt the remaining butter and stir in the flour. Cook over low heat for 2 minutes, stirring constantly. Gradually add the milk, then egg yolks and lemon juice. Stir until smooth and very thick. Season with salt and pepper.

Add the shrimp and cheese to the sauce. Simmer over low heat until heated through. Add lobster mixture to sauce and mix well. Spoon into scallop shells or ramekins and top with bread crumbs. Bake for 15 minutes or until lightly browned.

Garnish with watercress and serve immediately.

Serves 6 to 8

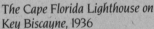

The Cape Florida Lighthouse on Key Biscayne, 1936

WILD RICE SEAFOOD CASSEROLE WITH OYSTER SAUCE

2 pints raw oysters or 1 pound cooked crab meat or shrimp

1-1/2 cups uncooked wild rice

3 cups beef broth

1/2 cup (1 stick) butter

3 cups Oyster Sauce

Preheat oven to 325 degrees.
Cook rice in 3 cups beef broth.
Drain oysters and reserve liquid for Oyster Sauce. Sauté oysters over moderate heat until edges curl. Drain.
Combine the cooked rice with butter and toss. Spoon 1/2 the wild rice in a baking dish and add the oysters, shrimp or crab meat. Add remaining rice and smooth out.
Cover casserole with Oyster Sauce and bake 30 minutes.

OYSTER SAUCE

2-1/2 tablespoons butter, divided in half

1-1/2 tablespoons flour

1 cup oyster liquor or oyster liquor and milk to make 1 cup.

Salt and pepper, to taste

2 tablespoons onions, finely chopped

1-1/2 cups large mushrooms, sliced

1/2 teaspoon curry powder

1/4 to 1/2 cup heavy cream

Heat half the butter in a saucepan and add flour, stirring with a wire whisk. Blend in the oyster liquor. When thickened and smooth, add salt and pepper.
Heat remaining butter and add the onions. When onions are soft, add the mushrooms and cook until juices form. Sprinkle with curry powder. Add the sauce and heavy cream and cook for about 5 minutes while stirring. Makes 3 cups sauce.

Serves 6 to 8

Note: If using crab meat or shrimp substitute 1 cup milk or cream for the oyster liquor.

POACHED YELLOWTAIL WITH GINGER SAUCE

1 whole yellowtail (2 to 2-1/2 pounds), cleaned

1 medium piece ginger, crushed

2 cloves garlic, chopped

1/3 cup salt

1 teaspoon pepper

1 teaspoon oil

2 tablespoons wine

1 tablespoon vinegar

In a poaching pan, half filled with water, add all ingredients except fish. Bring to a hard boil and add fish. Turn off heat immediately, cover and steam for 15 minutes.

Spoon poaching liquid over fish until it flakes easily with a fork. Reheat if necessary. Do not overcook. Remove fish to a heated platter.

GINGER SAUCE

1/3 cup sesame oil

2 cloves garlic

1 medium piece ginger, sliced

1/2 cup soy sauce

1/2 teaspoon sugar

1 teaspoon salt

1/2 teaspoon pepper

4 scallions, sliced (garnish)

5 Chinese mushrooms, soaked and slivered (garnish)

Bamboo shoots (garnish)

Heat oil in a small sauce pan, add garlic and ginger. Remove from heat and add remaining ingredients. Mix well and pour over the fish. Garnish with scallions, mushrooms and bamboo shoots.

Serves 2 to 3

T HE COMMODORE *Ralph Middleton Munroe loved Biscayne Bay.* He first came as a tourist in 1877, and was drawn by the purity of the air and water and the bravery and resourcefulness of the few settlers of the wilderness communities. When he moved to South Florida from Staten Island, he built his home, "The Barnacle," next door to the Peacock Inn in Coconut Grove. It was innovatively designed for comfortable tropical living, and is now a designated historic site.

He took an active part in community life. He arranged for the reopening of the Coconut Grove Post Office, investigated fish and turtle farming, sponging, pineapple and guava canning, sisal and lumber production and replanted thousands of coconut trees that had been destroyed by the 1876 hurricane. As a licensed salvor and shippers' agent he brought much needed flotsam and jetsam to shore. He formed the Biscayne Bay Yacht Club, donated land for the church, school and library and continued a lifelong career designing unique shallow-draft boats, comfortable, maneuverable and seaworthy enough for the Gulf Stream.

He was an active and farsighted ecologist. In his 70's he fought to get an injunction which stopped dredge-happy real estate speculators from filling Biscayne Bay with artificial islands.

Munroe had a rare gift for making and keeping friends and he kept up a lively correspondence with them all, usually extolling the virtues of life in Coconut Grove and often enclosing one of his excellent photographs.

SUMPTUOUS SEAFOOD WILD RICE

| 1/2 pound raw bay scallops |
| 4 pounds medium raw shrimp, shelled and deveined |
| 1 cup uncooked wild rice, washed and soaked |
| 1 can (8 ounces) water chestnuts, sliced |
| 1/2 pound small white mushroom caps |
| 1 can (14 ounces) hearts of palm, sliced |
| 1 jar (6 ounces) marinated artichoke hearts |
| 10 sprigs of parsley, finely chopped |
| 4 ounces pimentos, thinly sliced |
| 1 large red bell pepper, seeded and diced |
| 1 bunch green onions, chopped |
| Marie's Creamy Italian Dressing* |
| Salt and pepper, to taste |

Poach scallops gently until opaque. Drain. Do not overcook.

Shell and devein shrimp. Boil shrimp until pink. Drain

Cook wild rice per instructions on package.

Mix all ingredients together and refrigerate. The flavor is enhanced if made the day before. Add more dressing at serving time. Can be served hot or cold.

Serves 8 to 10

*Found in the produce section of a supermarket.

CHARLES AVENUE BAHAMIAN FISH STEW

| 2 hot peppers |
| 1 teaspoon salt |
| Key lime juice |
| 1 pound grouper, cut into chunks |
| 1/2 pound onions, sliced |
| 1/2 pound potatoes, sliced |
| 1/2 cup (1 stick) butter |

Make marinade by grinding hot peppers and salt in a mortar and pestle adding lime juice to make a paste. Spread on fish chunks. Let fish marinate for 20 minutes.

In a pot, layer fish chunks, onion slices and potato slices. Add water to within 1-inch of top of layered ingredients.

Add butter. Bring to a boil and when potatoes are tender serve.

Serves 4 to 6

BAKED MANGROVE SNAPPER GARNI

| 4 pounds Mangrove snapper fillets |
| 1 tablespoon oil |
| Salt and pepper, to taste |
| 1 tablespoon butter |
| 2 green peppers, seeded and sliced |
| 2 medium onions, sliced |
| 3 large tomatoes, sliced |
| 6 strips bacon |
| 1 package frozen peas (garnish) |
| 1 bunch parsley (garnish) |
| Lemon or lime slices (garnish) |

Preheat oven to 350 degrees.

Coat fish with oil, salt and pepper. Place in ovenproof dish which can be used as a serving dish.

Decorate fish with onions, peppers and tomatoes sautéed in butter. Top with bacon strips.

Bake approximately 1/2 hour or until done.

Put peas in boiling water until just heated, drain. Garnish fish with peas, parsley and decoratively cut lemon or lime slices.

Serves 6 to 8

CHINESE CASHEW STEAMED SNAPPER

| 1-1/2 pounds snapper fillets (or sea bass or sea trout) |
| 1 cup onions, very thinly sliced |
| 1 cup celery, very thinly sliced |
| 1 cup mushrooms, very thinly sliced |
| 1/2 cup salad oil |
| 1/2 cup raisins |
| 1/2 cup cashews, chopped |
| Scallions, chopped |
| Hot pickle rings, chopped |
| Chinese noodles |
| Tamari or soy sauce |

In a steamer, poach fillets about 10 minutes or until flaky. Mix onions, celery, and mushrooms. Remove fish to heated ovenproof platter and cover with the mixture.

Heat oil until smoking and pour over fish.

Garnish with raisins, nuts, scallions, hot pickles and noodles. Sprinkle with a dash of tamari.

Serves 4

FABULOUS FISHER ISLAND

The mangrove-covered tip of Miami Beach was once known as Rabbit Key. A small inlet was cut to make a channel for boats and the tides and currents enlarged it, thus creating a separate island. In 1917 the government dredged it deeper to make the ship channel, Government Cut.

William Vanderbilt, great-grandson of Cornelius, fell in love with the scrub-filled sandbar and traded his yacht "Eagle" to Carl Fisher, developer of Miami Beach, for seven acres. He later bought more land. The modest Vanderbilt preferred this area to the millionaire haunts of Palm Beach and Newport, and in the '20s he spent $1.5 million on his seaside hideaway. Named "Alva Base" after his 264-foot yacht, the beautiful Mediterranean-styled compound included an aviary, golf course, tennis courts and a hanger for his seaplane. Vanderbilt enjoyed his tropical paradise for twenty years.

Boat racer-inventor Gar Wood then bought it and in the fifties sold part of the land to an investment group headed by Charles (Bebe) Rebozo with the provision he could continue to live there, which he did for thirty years. It was sold again in 1979 and has been transformed into a $503 million resort community. The exquisite mansion has been restored as a clubhouse.

FISHER ISLAND BAKED FILLETS

2 pounds trout, dolphin, grouper or snapper fillets

Salt and pepper, to taste

5 tablespoons mayonnaise

3 tablespoons green onion or 1 medium onion, chopped

3 tablespoons fresh basil or dill, chopped

3 tablespoons lemon juice

Butter

Preheat oven to 350 degrees.
Wash and dry fish. Coat both sides of the fish with mayonnaise. Salt and pepper to taste. Place fish in a large buttered casserole dish or pan.
Sprinkle the fish with onions, herbs and lemon juice.
Bake for 25 to 30 minutes depending on the thickness of the fish fillets.

Serves 4

Souvenir postcard

1925
Douglass Entrance
to Coral Gables

CHICKEN CURRY VINDALOO

2 chickens, cut into pieces

Salt, to taste

2 large onions, finely chopped

4 tablespoons oil

1 teaspoon ground cumin

1 teaspoon ground ginger or 2 teaspoons curry powder

4 to 6 garlic cloves, crushed

Chili powder, to taste

1 can (6 ounces) tomato paste

Water or chicken stock

2 sticks cinnamon

1 cup malt vinegar

6 whole cloves

Wash and skin chicken. Put in a large pot and cover with salted water. Simmer 1 to 1-1/2 hours or until tender. Cool, discard bones. Cut meat into pieces and set aside.

In a large skillet, brown onions in oil. Add cumin, ginger or curry powder, garlic and chili powder. Stir in tomato paste, water or chicken stock, cinnamon, vinegar, chicken and cloves. Mix well and simmer 1 hour until meat is well seasoned. Add more vinegar or stock if necessary.

Serves 6 to 8

Note: A vindaloo is a dry curry and does not have a lot of sauce. Serve over rice with chutney.

LEMON CHICKEN

4 pounds chicken, cut into pieces

LEMON BASTING SAUCE

3/4 cup olive oil, finest quality

1/4 cup lemon juice

1/4 cup parsley, chopped

1 teaspoon salt

1 teaspoon garlic, crushed

1/4 teaspoon pepper

1 teaspoon oregano

1 teaspoon fresh basil

Preheat oven to 350 degrees.

Place chicken pieces in casserole, skin side down. Cover with basting sauce. Bake 30 minutes. Turn, baste again and bake 30 minutes longer.

Serves 6 to 8

LARKINS LOLLIPOP CHICKEN

Larkins was an active pioneer farming community. The name was changed to South Miami in 1926.

1 tablespoon white wine

2 cloves garlic, crushed

1/3 cup soy sauce

Dash of salt and pepper

1 tablespoon brown sugar

1 piece ginger root, crushed

24 chicken wings, drumstick only

1 cup flour

4 cups peanut oil

Combine first 6 ingredients and mix thoroughly.

Push meat toward large end of drumstick. Marinate drumsticks at least 1 hour. Drain and reshape if necessary.

Flour drumsticks and deep fry in very hot oil until brown, approximately 10 minutes. Drain on paper towels.

Serves 8 to 10

SZECHWAN CHICKEN

8 boneless chicken breast halves, slightly flattened

3 tablespoons sesame oil

1 teaspoon garlic, crushed

3 slices fresh ginger root

4 tablespoons hoisin sauce

1/4 cup sherry

Dash of dried chili pepper flakes, to taste (optional)

1 cup scallions, chopped (garnish)

1 cup peanuts (garnish)

In a large skillet, sauté chicken, garlic and ginger in sesame oil. Cook chicken 4 minutes on each side, remove ginger. Add hoisin sauce, sherry and chili pepper flakes. Cook 2 minutes.

Garnish with chopped scallions and peanuts.

Serves 8

Note: To use as an appetizer, cut chicken into small pieces and serve on toothpicks.

SUNSHINE CHICKEN WITH POACHED ORANGES

1 teaspoon salt

1/4 teaspoon pepper, freshly ground

1 teaspoon basil

8 broiler-fryer chicken thighs

8 broiler-fryer chicken drumsticks

1/2 cup soy sauce

1/2 cup catsup

1/4 cup honey

1/4 cup corn oil

2 cloves garlic, crushed

Preheat oven to 350 degrees.

In a bowl mix soy sauce, catsup, honey, oil and garlic.

Sprinkle chicken with salt, pepper and basil. Place chicken in a single layer in a shallow baking pan. Baste with sauce. Bake uncovered, basting frequently, 45 minutes or until a fork can be inserted easily. Remove to serving platter and garnish with Poached Oranges.

Combine the remaining basting sauce with sauce from Poached Oranges and serve in a separate bowl.

POACHED ORANGES

3/4 cup water

1-1/2 cups sugar

6 Navel oranges, peeled and cut into wedges

3 tablespoons orange rind, slivered

2 tablespoons orange liqueur

In a saucepan over medium heat, cook sugar and orange rind in water until slightly thickened, about 8 minutes.

Place orange wedges in the syrup. Reduce heat and cook on low until warm. Remove from heat. Add liqueur and chill.

Serves 6 to 8

CHICKEN WITH TARRAGON

2 to 2 1/2 pound chicken, split in half for broiling, saving backbone, gizzard, liver, heart and neck

Salt and pepper, to taste

2 tablespoons butter

2 tablespoons shallots, finely chopped

2 teaspoons fresh tarragon, finely chopped or 1 teaspoon dried tarragon

1/2 cup dry white wine

1/4 cup water

Sprinkle the chicken with salt and pepper. Heat the butter in a heavy skillet large enough to hold the chicken. Cook chicken skin side down, surrounded by the gizzard, liver, heart, neck and backbone, until golden brown. Turn and cook 5 minutes longer. Remove all chicken pieces and set aside.

Cook shallots briefly. Add the tarragon and wine. Stir to dissolve the brown particles on the bottom of the skillet. Stir in the water.

Return chicken to the skillet, skin side up, and cover. Cook about 20 minutes or until the chicken is thoroughly tender and nicely glazed.

Serves 4

Home on the Florida Keys

HONEY AND TAR COUGH "CURE"
Put one tablespoon liquid tar into a shallow tin dish and place it in boiling water until the tar is hot. To this add a pint of extracted honey and stir well for half an hour, adding to it a level teaspoonful pulverized borax. Keep well corked in a bottle. Dose – teaspoonful every one, two or three hours, according to severity of the cough.
   – From an old church cookbook, specific origin unknown.

ZESTY CHICKEN PERU

1 fryer, cut up; or 1 boiling hen, left whole

2 whole onions

Salt and pepper, to taste

2 medium onions, diced

Olive oil

3 slices bread

1/2 cup milk

2 small cans tomato sauce

2 teaspoons chili powder

1/2 teaspoon chili pepper, crushed

Juice of 1 orange

1 cup Parmesan cheese, grated

Black pepper, freshly ground

1/2 to 1 cup walnuts, chopped (garnish)

Preheat oven to 350 degrees.

Put chicken in large pot and cover with water, adding 2 whole onions, salt and pepper. Cook until tender.

In the meantime, sauté the onions in a little olive oil until nicely browned. Set aside.

In an ample casserole soak bread in milk and mash well. Add tomato sauce, chili powder, chili peppers and onions. Add the cooked chicken. (If using fryer, add the cut up pieces; if using a boiling hen, shred meat from bones.) Stir well, covering chicken with the sauce. Add orange juice. Sprinkle with cheese and black pepper.

Bake in oven until bubbly. Sprinkle with nuts and serve with rice. If chicken gets dry during baking, add chicken stock.

Serves 4 to 6

PAT'S POULET WITH CRÈME FRAÎCHE

CRÈME FRAÎCHE

1/2 cup sour cream

1/2 cup heavy cream

Using a whisk, thoroughly blend sour cream and heavy cream in a bowl. Cover loosely and allow to stand in a warm place until thickened; this may take 12 hours or longer.

Cover tightly and refrigerate for at least 4 hours; the crème should then be very thick.

PAT'S POULET

8 chicken breast halves, skinned and boned

Flour

Salt and pepper

1/2 cup (1 stick) butter

2 shallots, chopped

3/4 cup white wine

1/4 cup Calvados or Apple Jack

3/4 cup Crème Fraîche

1/4 teaspoon Herbes de Provence (or thyme)

Dredge chicken breasts in flour, salt and pepper. In large skillet sauté shallots. Add chicken and cook on both sides until done.

Remove chicken from pan to ovenproof serving platter. Add white wine and cook down for about 2 minutes. Add Calvados or Apple Jack. Cook until very hot. Pour over chicken, and if you wish, flambé. Cover chicken with Crème Fraîche.

Serve with Granny Smith apples, peeled, cored, cut into sections and sautéed in butter.

Serves 8

LADIES DON'T SWEAT – THEY GLOW

Pity the well-born, delicately nurtured Florida pioneer lady. Imagine if you will an August afternoon in the 1890's, the sun is high, the breeze is still, the temperature is nearly 90.

The lady of the house has just returned from a meeting of the Housekeeper's Club. She is most appropriately dressed in a long sleeved, high neck floral frock, hat and gloves. Her, ahem, underthings include a full-length cotton petticoat and a corset with a small bustle attachment. Her stockings are lisle or cotton and the shoes are high topped.

If she even considered bathing in Biscayne Bay, she would remember that Queen Victoria mandated twelve yards of serge for her bathing costume.

If she is newly arrived, her furniture is most likely black oak, ponderously carved, covered in damask trimmed with tassels. The Victorian times were known for their moral rigidity, excessive ornamentation and modesty.

Those were hard times for the overdressed. You've come a long way, Florida lady.

SESAME CHICKEN IN CUMBERLAND SAUCE

2 cups bread crumbs

1/4 cup sesame seeds

1/2 cup Parmesan cheese, grated

1/4 cup parsley, chopped

1 teaspoon pepper

6 boneless chicken breast halves, skinned, pounded to 1/4 inch

2 tablespoons butter, melted

CUMBERLAND SAUCE

3 large oranges, rind and juice

3 large lemons, rind and juice

1 cup red currant jelly

2 tablespoons Port wine

2 teaspoons Dijon-style mustard

Salt and pepper, to taste

Preheat oven to 400 degrees.

Combine first 5 ingredients in bowl, blend well. Dip chicken in
butter and coat with sesame breading. Place in baking pan and bake for
20 minutes.

While chicken cooks, grate oranges and lemons. Squeeze juice into a
bowl. Place peel in saucepan, cover with cold water. Bring to a boil.
Drain. Boil and drain again and set aside.

Combine juice with remaining ingredients and heat. Stir in grated
peel, season to taste. Pour over cooked chicken.

Serves 6

DOROTHY'S OWN TURKEY CHILI

5 pounds yellow onions, chopped

4 stalks of celery, chopped

1 green bell pepper, seeded and chopped

Oil for sautéing

2 pounds turkey, ground

2 cloves garlic, crushed

Salt and freshly ground pepper, to taste

2 cans (28 ounces each) tomatoes, chopped

1 can beer, or more if you like

3-1/2 tablespoons cumin

3 tablespoons chili powder

2 cans (19 ounces each) kidney beans

Sauté onions, celery and bell pepper. Sauté turkey until white. Place all ingredients except beans in a large kettle and simmer 45 minutes. Add beans the final 15 minutes.

Serve over large slices of lettuce. Top with chopped onions and Cheddar cheese. Serve with sour dough bread, sweet butter and cold beer.

Serves 20

CORNISH GAME HENS STUFFED WITH SPICED PEACHES

This recipe served hot with wild rice makes an elegant dinner. For a fabulous picnic, arrange chilled cornish hens on a platter and surround with green seedless grapes.

4 Cornish game hens (thaw 24 hours ahead)

2 large cans spiced peaches

1/2 cup (1 stick) butter

Salt and pepper, to taste

Preheat oven to 325 degrees.

Remove giblets. Sprinkle inside and out with salt and pepper. Stuff with spiced peaches. Place on rack in open baking pan and bake 45 minutes to 1 hour, basting with melted butter and peach juice every 15 minutes.

Serves 4

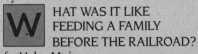

WHAT WAS IT LIKE FEEDING A FAMILY BEFORE THE RAILROAD?

by Helen Muir

Well, it wasn't easy if one is thinking in terms of supermarkets and lavish selections of food from every part of the globe.

But it wasn't that hard, either, if one happened to be tuned to the land and the sea and to sharing and helping one another.

In Miami USA I wrote about these things and how the women coped. "They learned to use guava syrup as the principal sweetening for pies and cakes. They made johnnycake ... sweet and plenty of it, stewed venison, ash-baked sweet potatoes, roast hog, gypsy stew (usually made from wild hog, turtle or manatee), coontie pudding and coontie pancakes.

"Their children never saw milk but they ate Indian sofkee for gruel and boiled Seminole squash, reef bean soup, turtle fry and fried chicken.

"Most families had a few chickens, but they paid the price by fighting off 'coons, wildcats and 'possums. If they planted vegetables, the deer and rabbits became their enemies. What with wild duck and quail in the hammocks, there was always plenty to eat. The women made good use of fruits like the hog plum, coco plum, seagrape and custard apple as well as sapodillas, guavas, limes and few pomegranates ..."

TARRAGON CORNISH GAME HENS

6 Cornish game hens (thaw for 24 hours)

6 garlic cloves, whole

3 tablespoons fresh tarragon, chopped

1-1/2 teaspoons salt

3/4 teaspoon white pepper

2 teaspoons garlic salt

3/4 cup dry white wine

3/4 cup (1-1/2 sticks) butter, melted

Preheat oven to 400 degrees.

In each thawed hen place 1 clove garlic, 1 teaspoon tarragon, 1/4 teaspoon salt, 1/8 teaspoon pepper. Sprinkle outside of hen with garlic salt and refrigerate, 6 hours or more.

Cook hens on rack, breast side up, for 45 minutes to 1 hour. Baste often with melted butter mixed with wine and 1 tablespoon tarragon. Remove from oven and make sauce.

SAUCE

1 chicken bouillon cube or granules

1/2 cup milk, warmed

1/4 cup sherry

2 tablespoons flour

1/4 cup mushrooms, sliced

Reserve 2 tablespoons of pan drippings. Add chicken bouillon dissolved in warm milk and sherry. Sprinkle with 2 tablespoons flour to thicken. Add mushrooms and seasonings. Simmer until mushrooms are tender.

Serves 6 to 8

HEARTY CASSOULET

3 cups partially cooked duck or goose, cut into serving pieces

1 pound dried pea beans

6 tablespoons parsley, chopped

3 large bay leaves

1 teaspoon thyme

6 cloves garlic, chopped

1 celery stalk, chopped

Salt and pepper

2 Italian sausages

2 medium onions, chopped

1/2 cup tomato sauce

1 cup white wine

1/2 pound cooked ham, cut up

Soak dried beans in cold water overnight.

Drain the beans and cover with cold water. Add 3 tablespoons parsley, bay leaves, thyme, celery, salt, pepper and garlic. Cook slowly 1 hour. Strain and reserve liquid.

Fry Italian sausages; remove from pan and set aside.

Pour off almost all the fat and cook onions until golden brown. Stir in tomato sauce, remaining parsley and wine.

In large earthenware casserole put layer of cooked beans. Add a layer of the fowl, some sausage slices and part of the tomato sauce and wine mixture. Continue layering in same manner, ending with the beans. Cover with the reserved bean liquid. Place lid on casserole and bake in slow oven (250 degrees) for 2 hours. If it gets too dry, add a little water.

Place pieces of ham on top of casserole ingredients and bake uncovered an additional 30 minutes.

Serves 6 to 8

"The schooner from Key West, which every six weeks picked up the coontie starch, also brought groceries so that the operation amounted to barter. A man could get along fine without ever seeing cash. If he found himself with a pocketful of cash he celebrated by buying jawbreakers for the children when the Key West schooner dropped anchor.

"If you felt like eating venison but didn't feel like killing a deer you might effect a barter with an Indian. Fifty oranges was considered a fair exchange for half a deer. Twenty-five would bring a couple of hams. If a man had a bit of luck and ran into a school of kingfish on the Cape Florida sand-bores or off Bear Cut buoy, he would lay aboard all he could hold and sail home blowing the conch shell to call the settlers to come and share the haul."

That was a long time ago. Today the Friends of the Miami-Dade Public Library is working through a Culinary Committee toward making the Phillip Johnson designed main library at the downtown cultural center a place for spotlighting tropical and subtropical foods, including those which have been overlooked in the race toward the development of South Florida.

SAUTÉED YOUNG DOVE OR QUAIL

Dove or quail

Milk

Salt and pepper, to taste

Flour

Butter for sautéing

Dip birds in milk. Sprinkle with flour, salt and pepper. Sauté in 1/2-inch hot butter, turning once until done.

GRAVY

1 tablespoon flour

2 tablespoons butter, melted

1 cup cream

Salt and pepper, to taste

Add flour to butter and slowly add cream, salt and pepper.

TINDALL'S SMOKED TURKEY

12 to 14 pound turkey, rubbed with seasoned salt

Charcoal (12-1/2 pound bag)

Dome-shaped charcoal smoker

Log of hickory, 4 x 10-inches, chopped into sticks

1 cup sherry

Light a heaping pile of charcoal in the lower pan of the smoker. When the coals are glowing, cover them with hickory sticks. Put sherry into the water pan and add water to fill. Place it above the fire.

Put the turkey on the rack above the water pan and cover with the lid. Four hours later re-charge the fire with additional hickory. Turkey should be ready after 10 hours.

Serves 12

. . . .

VICKIE'S QUAIL

Quail, split

Lime juice

Salt and pepper, to taste

Flour

Butter

Marinate quail in lime juice, salt and pepper for 1 to 2 hours. Dust with flour, salt and pepper. Brown in butter.

One or two birds per person

One or two birds per person

MEAT AND GAME

Plymouth
Congregational
Church
1916

VEGETABLE INGREDIENTS

for Beef Bourguignonne

2-1/2 cups white mushrooms, quartered

3 tablespoons butter, melted

1 teaspoon lemon juice

Salt and pepper, to taste

Cooked salt pork strips

12 small white boiler onions, peeled and blanched

1 tablespoon granulated sugar

2 tablespoons parsley, chopped

Sauté mushrooms in 1 tablespoon butter, add lemon juice, salt and pepper. Cook for 3 minutes. Remove from pan. In same skillet, sauté onions in 2 tablespoons butter; sprinkle with sugar. Shake until browned.

Stir vegetables into meat and cook 35 minutes, serve.

Serves 9 to 12

BOEUF BOURGUIGNONNE

6 ounces lean salt pork, trimmed, cut into 3/4-inch strips

3 pounds stew beef, cut into 1-inch cubes

1/4 cup Cognac or good brandy

2 teaspoons garlic, finely chopped

2 teaspoons tomato paste

1 teaspoon beef extract (Bovril or BV)

1/2 cup red Burgundy wine

1/4 cup each Madeira wine and dry sherry

1 cup each chicken stock and beef stock

2 tablespoons currant jelly

Freshly ground black pepper, to taste

2 tablespoons cornstarch dissolved in 1/2 cup stock

Preheat oven to 300 degrees.

Blanch salt pork in boiling water. Simmer 5 minutes; drain. In Dutch oven, brown salt pork until crisp; set aside to use with vegetables. Drain 1/2 of the fat, saving 1/2 for later use.

In the Dutch oven, sauté the beef in pork fat, browning a few cubes at a time on all sides; set aside. When all the beef has been browned, return to Dutch oven.

Pour heated brandy over the beef and ignite carefully. Remove beef, leaving juices. Sauté garlic in juices. Remove pan from heat; stir in tomato paste and beef extract. Return to heat. Add Burgundy, Madeira, sherry, stock, jelly and pepper. Stir over moderate heat until mixture comes to a boil.

Blend sauce with meat in Dutch oven; cover. Braise in oven 1-1/2 hours or until meat is tender. Add the vegetable ingredients 35 minutes before the end of cooking time. Stir in cornstarch mixture 10 minutes before serving.

Serves 9 to 12

STANDING RIB ROAST WITH YORKSHIRE PUDDING

Standing rib roast, 4 ribs or more

Garlic powder, or slivers of fresh garlic

4 to 5 small onions, peeled

4 tablespoons (1/2 stick) butter

4 to 6 tablespoons flour

1 tablespoon Kitchen Bouquet

4 to 6 cups water

Preheat oven to 450 degrees.

Sprinkle roast with garlic powder or insert slivers of fresh garlic in fat. Place bone side down on rack in roaster pan with onions.

Place in 450 degree oven. Immediately turn oven to 325 degrees and roast 20 minutes per pound for medium rare (150 degrees on meat thermometer). When beef is done, remove to serving platter.

To make gravy, pour off fat, retaining the juices. Add butter to pan and place over 2 burners. Add flour to make roux. Brown nicely and add water while whisking. Add Kitchen Bouquet, salt and pepper to taste. Simmer 4 minutes.

Serve roast surrounded by squares of Yorkshire Pudding. (Pudding should go into the oven when roast comes out.) Serve with gravy.

There are 2 to 3 servings to each pound of rib roast.

YORKSHIRE PUDDING
for Standing Rib Roast

1 cup flour

1 cup milk

3 eggs

3/4 teaspoon salt

1/2 cup (1 stick) butter or 1/2 cup pan drippings

Preheat oven to 450 degrees.

Blend the first 4 ingredients well. Refrigerate for 30 minutes.

In oven, heat butter or drippings in skillet or 8 x 8-inch pan, until it sizzles, about 2 minutes. Add batter. Bake 20 to 25 minutes or until puffed high and brown. Serve immediately.

Note: A 10-inch skillet or a 9 x 13-inch pan will hold 2 units of this recipe.

CASHEW-CARAMBOLA STIR FRY

2 to 3 tablespoons peanut oil

1-inch slice ginger, finely minced

1 pound sirloin steak, thinly sliced*

1/2 medium red pepper, cut into julienne

4 green onions, sliced diagonally (include 2 inches of green)

3 tablespoons soy sauce

3 carambolas, seeds removed, thinly sliced

1/2 cup cashews, lightly toasted

Toasted coconut, to taste (optional)

Heat oil in a hot wok or frying pan. Add ginger and steak, stirring quickly, for 1 minute. Add red pepper and green onions; stir for 2 minutes. Add soy sauce, carambolas and cashews; stir quickly.

Garnish with toasted coconut and serve over steamed rice.

Serves 4 to 6

*Sirloin is easier to slice when partially frozen.

STEAK DIANE

6 tablespoons butter

1 teaspoon fresh garlic, finely minced

1 teaspoon shallots, chopped

4 slices (4 ounces each) beef sirloin

Salt and pepper, to taste

3 medium fresh mushrooms, sliced thinly

3 ounces red wine

3 ounces Bordelaise sauce*

2 ounces brandy

Scallions, chopped (garnish)

Watercress (garnish)

Lightly sauté garlic and shallots in butter. Add the steaks sprinkled with salt and pepper moving them around in the pan and against the edges to pick up the garlic. Cook until rare (approximately 2-1/2 minutes). Remove from the pan.

Add mushrooms to pan, scraping the bottom as they are sautéed. Stir in wine and Bordelaise Sauce. Reduce sauce by half.

Return steaks to pan. Add the brandy and flambé. After the steaks have been cooked as desired, cover with sauce. Garnish with raw scallions and watercress.

Serves 2 to 4

*Bordelaise Sauce (See Index.)

SUKIYAKI

3 tablespoons oil

1 medium onion, thinly sliced

4 large mushrooms, sliced

1/2 pound sirloin tip or eye round beef, thinly sliced

1/4 pound spinach, washed, dried, torn into 1-inch pieces

4 scallions, thinly sliced

3 stalks celery, sliced diagonally

4 tablespoons soy sauce

2 tablespoons sugar

5-1/4 ounces beef consommé, canned

1 cup rice, cooked

In a skillet over medium high heat, sauté onion, mushrooms and beef in oil. Add spinach, scallions and celery; stir fry.

Add soy sauce, sugar and consommé. Cook for 2 minutes, stirring often. Do not overcook vegetables.

Serve over hot rice.

Serves 4

The Japanese provide each guest with a small bowl containing 1 beaten raw egg. Each bite is dipped into the egg before eating.

MADRAS BEEF CURRY

2 tablespoons cooking oil

4 large onions, chopped

4 pounds beef chuck, cut into small cubes

2 cups dry red wine

1 large can tomatoes, chopped

2 teaspoons salt

2 tablespoons coriander

2 sticks cinnamon

2 teaspoons red pepper flakes

2 bell peppers, chopped

1 clove garlic, chopped

1 large can green peas, drained

White or brown rice, cooked

Brown onion in oil in a large Dutch oven or casserole.

Brown beef on all sides a few cubes at a time. Remove when browned. When all beef has been cooked, return meat to pot.

Add next 7 ingredients and cook 1 hour, covered, until beef is almost tender. Add garlic and green peas and cook 1/2 hour more. Remove cinnamon sticks.

Serve over rice. Offer a variety of condiments such as mango chutney, chopped onion, chopped peanuts, raisins, coconut, chopped egg yolks, etc.

Serves 8 to 10

The most popular alligator in town

POT-AU-FEU

This dish is traditional in France. It is served every Wednesday, or so they say.

4 pounds rump roast	3 carrots
4 pounds beef bones	2 tablespoons salt
4 1/2 cups water	1 bay leaf
4 peppercorns	
1 onion, stuck with 3 cloves	
4 to 5 leeks, well washed	
1 stalk celery	
1 turnip	
Sprig parsley	
1 teaspoon thyme, fresh	
2 1/2 pounds chicken pieces	
6 potatoes, quartered	
6 carrots	
1 head of cabbage, coarsely sliced (optional)	
18 to 20 tiny white onions (garnish)	
1 teaspoon sugar	

Put rump roast and beef bones in large soup pot with 4 cups of water, 3 carrots and next 9 ingredients. Cook gently for 2 hours, removing froth as it accumulates on the surface.

Add chicken to soup pot. Continue cooking until meat and fowl are tender, about 1 hour. One half hour before serving, add potatoes, 6 carrots, and cabbage if desired.

Meanwhile, brown tiny white onions in sugar and butter and let them cook until soft. Shake the pan often, so they will cook evenly.

To serve this in the French manner, serve broth in deep soup bowl with crusty rolls, tiny onions and horseradish, followed by sliced meat, fowl and vegetables.

Serves 12 to 14

CALLE OCHO PICADILLO

1/4 teaspoon oregano

1/2 teaspoon salt

1/4 teaspoon pepper, freshly ground

1 clove of garlic, crushed

1/2 teaspoon celery seed

1/4 teaspoon paprika

2 medium onions, diced

2 large green peppers, diced

4 tablespoons olive oil

1-1/2 pounds ground beef

Large can tomatoes, crushed

2 tablespoons Worcestershire sauce

1/2 cup stuffed olives, drained (save 1/4 cup olive liquid)

1 small jar capers

1 cup seedless raisins

Combine first 6 ingredients.

Sauté onions and peppers in 2 tablespoons olive oil; set aside.

Sauté meat in 2 tablespoons olive oil; stir in seasonings, add tomatoes and Worcestershire sauce.

Combine all ingredients, cover and cook for about 35 minutes over low heat.

Serves 6 to 8

CALLE OCHO
Once merely an eastern extension of the Tamiami Trail, Southwest Eighth Street is now better known as "Calle Ocho," synonymous with the vibrant Cuban flavor of Miami and the heart of the area known as Little Havana.

Since 1959, when Fidel Castro led the Communist coup in Cuba, many of its citizens have been forced to flee. Because of business opportunities, climate, and cultural ties, Miami is the natural spot for the displaced Cubans to relocate.

A stroll along the busy sidewalks of Calle Ocho is like a visit to another country. Spanish is not only spoken but it is on the signs and in the air. The smells of the wonderful fresh bread, roasting pork, onions and garlic, fried bananas and fresh brewed coffee plus the sounds of the fast-paced Latin beat will immerse one in the exciting Hispanic culture.

The pace is quieter in Domino Park where the older men gather to discuss the topics of the day and play their favorite game of Dominos.

Carnaval, Miami's annual ten day festival, was begun to promote ethnic understanding in the community and has quickly become the largest Hispanic celebration in the United States. It concludes with an open house along Calle Ocho which attracts hundreds of thousands of people as much for the food as for the entertainment.

OLÉ TAMALE PIE

1 1/2 pounds ground chuck

1 1/2 ounces water

6 ounces tomato paste

1 envelope chili seasoning mix

1/4 cup ripe olives, diced

1/2 teaspoon sugar

In large skillet over medium heat, brown meat. Skim off fat. Stir in water, tomato paste, chili seasoning mix, diced olives and sugar. Cook, stirring until blended.

CORN MEAL MIXTURE

1 cup boiling water

1 cup yellow corn meal

1 teaspoon salt

1 cup cheddar cheese, shredded

1/2 cup corn chips, coarsely broken

Preheat oven to 350 degrees.

In medium saucepan combine corn meal, boiling water and salt. Cook corn meal mixture until thickened, stirring constantly. Spoon into 8 x 8 or 6 x 10-inch baking dish.

Spread meat mixture evenly over corn meal mixture; sprinkle with cheese and corn chips. Bake for 30 minutes. Cool 5 minutes before serving.

Serves 6 to 8

SOUTH AMERICAN SHEPHERDS' PIE

1-1/2 pounds ground beef

1/2 pound ground pork

2 eggs, lightly beaten

1/2 cup dry bread crumbs

3 tablespoons butter

1/2 cup green pepper, finely chopped

3/4 cup onions, finely chopped

2 cloves garlic, minced

1 tablespoon Worcestershire sauce

1/4 teaspoon Tabasco

1/2 teaspoon cayenne pepper

Salt and freshly ground black pepper, to taste

1/2 teaspoon cumin, ground

1/2 teaspoon thyme, crushed

1 teaspoon white pepper

Preheat oven to 450 degrees.

In a bowl, combine meats, eggs and bread crumbs. In a 12-inch frying pan, sauté peppers, onions and garlic in butter for 5 minutes. Add to meat mixture with seasonings and mix well.

Bake for 30 minutes in a 9 x 13-inch pan. Pour off drippings; reserve 2-1/2 tablespoons for vegetable mixture.

Serves 6 to 8

MASHED POTATOES
for South American Shepherds' Pie

2 pounds potatoes, peeled, diced, boiled and mashed with 1/2 cup evaporated milk and 3 tablespoons butter

Salt and pepper, to taste

VEGETABLE TOPPING
for South American Shepherds' Pie

1-1/2 cups carrots, grated

1 cup onion, chopped

1-1/2 cups zucchini, cut into julienne

1 cup yellow squash, cut into julienne

Salt and pepper, to taste

Dash cayenne pepper

Preheat oven to 525 degrees.

Sauté carrots and onions in 2-1/2 tablespoons drippings saved from the meat mixture for 2 minutes. Add zucchini and squash. Sauté, stirring constantly, 3 to 4 minutes.

Mound sautéed vegetables on top of meat loaf, top with mashed potatoes. Bake 8 to 10 minutes until brown on top.

Serves 6 to 8

THE VENETIAN POOL
The unique historic landmark, Venetian Pool in Coral Gables, was designed by the creative Denman Fink to take advantage of a huge quarry which remained after coral rock was taken for building homes. Opened in 1924, it is an imaginative mix of "hidden" caves and natural diving platforms. The spacious pool areas are filled with spring water from an artesian well and surrounded by a fanciful structure with towers, archways and patios. Tourists and local families alike have enjoyed the uncommon Old World atmosphere of the Venetian Pool for over half a century.

A perfect setting for beauty contests of the day, it was also the locale of frequent afternoon tea dances and evening dances on its patios. On occasion, with the pool drained (it was drained and filled every day), a symphony orchestra seated on its floor would send strains of music up to a poolside audience.

In a promotional publication of the day, the Venetian Pool and Casino, as it was known, was described: "Pergola-covered tiled terrace for afternoon tea and a patio floored with terrazzo for dancing. The effect is one of festivity and color with the decorated gondola mooring posts as in Venice, and the miniature island of coconut palms reached by a graceful footbridge."

VENETIAN VEAL SCALLOPINI

1 pound veal, thinly sliced

1 to 2 teaspoons fresh rosemary or 1/2 to 1 teaspoons dried

1 cup dry white wine

3 tablespoons flour, seasoned with salt and pepper

1/2 cup (1 stick) butter

Place veal between 2 sheets of wax paper and pound with a wooden mallet until flat and thin.

Dust with seasoned flour and sprinkle with rosemary; brown in butter. Remove veal from pan. Deglaze pan with wine, stirring up all the brown bits. Return meat to the pan and simmer one minute.

Serve with sautéed mushrooms and hot noodles.

Serves 4

Paul Whiteman's Orchestra in the 1920's swim of things, Venetian Pool, Coral Gables

VITELLO TONNATO

2 garlic cloves, slivered

3 anchovy fillets, cut into 1-inch pieces

3 to 3-1/2 pounds veal roast, top round

1 quart chicken stock

2 cups dry white wine

2 cups water

2 onions, coarsely chopped

2 carrots, chopped

3 celery stalks, chopped

2 bay leaves

6 parsley sprigs

10 whole peppercorns

Insert garlic and anchovies into small cuts in the veal. In a large heavy saucepan cover veal with boiling water and cook for 1 minute. Remove veal from pan and rinse with cold water. Discard water.

In the same pan, place veal and all the other ingredients. Add enough stock to cover and simmer approximately 2 hours or until tender. Let veal cool in the stock, covered, in refrigerator for 3 to 4 hours.

TUNA SAUCE
for Vitello Tonnato

3/4 cup olive oil

1 egg yolk

3 ounces tuna in oil

4 anchovy fillets, washed

2 tablespoons lemon juice

1/4 cup heavy cream

1/4 to 1/2 cup cooled stock

Salt and pepper, to taste

2 tablespoons small capers, rinsed (garnish)

In a blender, purée olive oil, egg yolk, tuna, anchovies and lemon juice. Pour into a small bowl. Slowly stir in cream. Add stock a little at a time until it looks creamy. Add capers and season to taste.

After veal has cooled, discard stock and vegetables. Slice veal very thinly. Spread a small amount of sauce on the bottom of a large platter. Place sliced veal on the platter and cover with remaining sauce. Wrap in plastic and refrigerate overnight or longer.

At least 1 hour before serving, take out of the refrigerator and bring to room temperature.

Serves 9 to 12

Serves 9 to 12

Welcome to Vizcaya

VEAL MARENGO

1/2 cup oil

4 pounds veal shoulder, cubed

1 cup onions, chopped

1 cup celery, chopped

1 clove garlic, crushed

1 cup dry white wine

2 cups tomato sauce

2 bay leaves

1 teaspoon oregano

1/2 teaspoon rosemary

2 teaspoons salt

1/2 teaspoon pepper

2 sprigs parsley, chopped

1 pound mushrooms, sliced

2 tablespoons lemon juice

1/4 cup (1/2 stick) butter

1 tablespoon flour

Heat oil in a Dutch oven or a large skillet. Brown veal turning often. Remove when brown. Do not over cook.

In same pan, sauté onion, celery and garlic, stirring until golden. Stir in 1/2 cup wine, tomato sauce, bay leaves, oregano, rosemary, parsley, salt and pepper. Return veal to pan. Bring to boil; reduce heat and simmer, covered, for 1-1/2 hours or until veal is tender. Remove bay leaves.

When veal has cooked 1-1/4 hours, toss mushrooms with lemon juice. Sauté in butter until tender.

Add remaining 1/2 cup of wine and mushrooms to veal mixture. Add flour mixed with 2 tablespoons water. Simmer covered for 15 minutes longer.

Serve over white rice.

Serves 10 to 12

VEAL Á LA VIZCAYA

1 carrot

1 celery stalk

2 onions, chopped (for broth)

1 onion, chopped (for browning)

2 pounds prime stewing veal, cut into small pieces

1 quart cold water

1/2 cup (1 stick) butter

1 pound mushrooms, sliced

1/2 cup heavy cream

1/4 teaspoon cornstarch

Salt and pepper, to taste

1 ounce sherry

Parsley (garnish)

In a large saucepan, place veal, carrot, celery and 2 onions in water. Bring to a boil slowly. Simmer gently for 1 hour, removing froth as it forms. Pour off the broth and set aside.

Brown the veal on all sides in butter in heavy saucepan. Add 1 chopped onion and lightly brown. Add mushrooms. Cover skillet and simmer for 20 minutes.

Mix cornstarch and cream. Combine with the veal, onions and mushrooms and stir well. Add sherry. Season to taste. If it gets too thick, thin with additional cream.

Bring just to boiling point and serve in vol-au-vent shell or a casserole. Sprinkle with parsley.

Serves 4 to 6

Note: The broth you set aside may be simmered with a bay leaf and served as the soup course.

The Everglades ... mysterious, unique, romantic, timeless. Its vast sheet of fresh water flows south over a thin limestone crust past tall sawgrass dotted with higher hammocks of hardwood trees. The soil is incredibly rich with years of decayed organic detritus 25 feet deep in places. Totally misunderstood until recent times, we now realize that the water supply furnished by the Everglades is far more important than the farmland that drainage would provide.

Zipping along the Tamiami Trail from Miami to Naples in an air-conditioned car, all seems serene and calm. It's fascinating to stop at a picnic area and listen and look at the abundance of life that calls this enchanting watery environment its home.

Imagine the difficulty of building this road in 1928 and what it was like to cross the Everglades before the road was built. Yet the Everglades have been home and sanctuary for a hundred years to the proud Indians who live there.

The sign at the reception center at Everglades National Park tells visitors that they have come to "a land of subtle charm and complexity preserved forever for the inspiration and enjoyment of mankind."

OSSO BUCO
(Braised Veal Shanks)

4 tablespoons (1/2 stick) butter	Flour
1 1/2 cups onion, finely chopped	1/2 cup olive oil
1/2 cup carrots, finely chopped	1 cup white wine
1/2 cup celery, finely chopped	3/4 cup beef or chicken stock
1 teaspoon garlic, finely chopped	
7 pounds veal shanks, 2 inches thick	
Salt and pepper, freshly ground (to taste)	
1 teaspoon fresh basil, chopped or 1/2 teaspoon dried	
1 teaspoon fresh thyme, chopped or 1/2 teaspoon dried	
3 cups tomatoes, drained and coarsely chopped	
6 parsley sprigs	
2 bay leaves	
1 tablespoon lemon peel, grated (garnish)	
3 tablespoons parsley, chopped (garnish)	

Preheat oven to 350 degrees.

In a Dutch oven, sauté onions, carrots, celery and garlic in butter for 10 to 15 minutes.

Season veal with salt and pepper, and roll in flour. Heat 6 tablespoons olive oil in heavy skillet; brown the veal. Add more oil as needed.

Remove veal from skillet, place in Dutch oven and discard oil. On high setting deglaze skillet with wine and reduce to 1/2 cup. Stir in stock, basil, thyme, tomatoes, parsley and bay leaves and bring to a boil. Pour over the veal, return to boil. Cover and bake in lower third of the oven 1 1/4 hours or until tender. Discard parsley and bay leaves.

To serve, arrange the veal on a heated platter and spoon the sauce and vegetables over and around it. Garnish with grated lemon and chopped parsley.

Serves 6 to 8

Note: This is wonderful served with Risotto alla Milanese. (See Index.)

SWEETBREADS AND MUSHROOMS IN CREAM

4 pounds veal sweetbreads

1/4 cup lemon juice

1 tablespoon salt

2 tablespoons white vinegar

1-1/2 cups (3 sticks) butter

2 pounds mushrooms, sliced

1/4 cup flour

2 cups chicken stock or broth

2 egg yolks

1 cup heavy cream

1/4 cup sherry

Salt and white pepper, to taste

Paprika (garnish)

Parsley, chopped (garnish)

Soak sweetbreads in cold water for 3 hours. Change cold water every 1/2 hour. The last hour add 1/4 cup lemon juice. Drain and remove connective tissue. Cover again with cold water in a saucepan, adding white vinegar and 1 tablespoon salt. Simmer 20 minutes. Drain and rinse in cold water. Place between sheets of wax paper and cover with cutting board to flatten, approximately 1 hour. Cut into 1/3-inch thick slices.

In a skillet sauté sweetbreads in 2 sticks of butter until lightly brown. Remove from pan. Add remaining butter less 3 tablespoons and sauté mushrooms until tender.

In a large saucepan melt 3 tablespoons butter and 1/4 cup flour. Stir 3 minutes. Add chicken stock, stirring until thickened. Remove from heat.

Beat egg yolks with heavy cream and add to sauce gradually. Add sherry, additional lemon juice, salt and pepper to taste.

Add the sweetbreads and mushrooms; simmer until hot.

Garnish with paprika and chopped parsley.

Serves 10 to 12

SOUTH OF FLAGLER CHILI

2 pounds ground chuck

2 onions, chopped

1 green pepper, chopped

1 can (38 ounces) Progresso tomatoes, crushed

1/2 teaspoon cumin

1 teaspoon oregano

2 bay leaves

3 tablespoons chili powder, or to taste

2 teaspoons salt

1 teaspoon pepper

2 cloves garlic

Brown meat in large heavy pot. Add onions and green pepper; cook until wilted. Add tomatoes and seasonings, heat to boil. Reduce heat and simmer about 2 hours. Skim fat as it rises.

GARNISH

1/2 pound extra sharp cheddar cheese, shredded

2 onions, finely chopped

4 hot peppers, chopped

Use any or all of the garnishes.

Serves 6 to 8

110

ROAST SADDLE OF LAMB WITH JULEP SAUCE

2 to 3-1/2 pound saddle of lamb, trimmed by the butcher

3/4 cup fresh bread crumbs

4 tablespoons (1/2 stick) butter, melted

2 tablespoons shallots, chopped

2 cloves garlic, crushed and chopped

1/4 cup parsley, chopped

1 cup brown stock

Tie lamb securely at least 3 times.

Preheat oven to 425 degrees.

Combine melted butter with shallots, garlic and parsley. Set aside.

Sear the lamb on all sides in a heavy ovenware pan, browning top first. Remove strings and sprinkle with herb mixture. Roast in a preheated oven about 35 minutes per pound for medium rare. Let stand 10 to 12 minutes before carving.

Discard fat accumulated in pan and add a cup of brown stock to the drippings. Boil 2 to 3 minutes scraping crusty bits into stock; strain. Serve with lamb.

Carve horizontally in thin slices, serve with Julep Sauce.

JULEP SAUCE

12 to 14 fresh mint leaves

1 tablespoon sugar

1 cup cider vinegar

Crush mint leaves in a small bowl. Add sugar and vinegar; mix well. Allow to steep.

Serves 6 to 10

FRENCH COUNTRY LEG OF LAMB

1 leg of lamb

1 tablespoon vegetable oil

Salt and pepper, to taste

1/2 teaspoon dried thyme

2 large cloves garlic, slivered

2 onions, cut in half

2 bay leaves

1 carrot, cut into pieces

1 cup water

Preheat oven to 425 degrees.

Have butcher remove and set aside hipbone of lamb. Discard skin, leaving a light layer of fat. Rub meat with oil; sprinkle with salt, pepper and thyme. Make gashes in the leg and insert the garlic.

Place leg, fat side down, on rack in a roasting pan, surround with the hipbone, onion halves, cut side down, bay leaves and carrot.

Bake for 1 hour. Remove and pour off fat. Return to pan, thick side up. Pour water in the pan and bake 30 minutes for medium-rare lamb (135 degrees inside temperature).

Discard hipbone and vegetables, cover with foil and let stand for 20 minutes before carving.

Serves 4 to 6

Note: This is delicious served with Flageolet Beans in Cream. (See Index.)

INDIAN LAMB AND LEMON STEW

(Sabji Ghorme)

Sabji Ghorme means "everybody at home," and is an ancient Indian delicacy.

2-1/2 pounds lamb, cut into 1-inch cubes

2 cups cold water

Salt and pepper, to taste

1 large onion, chopped

1/2 cup (1 stick) butter

10 bunches parsley, washed and chopped

3 bunches green onions, chopped

1-1/4 cups blackeyed peas, cooked

4-1/2 ounces lemon juice

Cover meat with 2 cups cold water, salted to taste. Cook over high heat until water begins to boil, reduce heat to medium for about 10 minutes, then to low. Continue cooking for about 1 hour until meat is tender and almost done. Drain and save stock.

Add the onion and butter to the meat. Sauté a few minutes, being careful that the lamb does not stick. If needed add some reserved stock.

Add the parsley, green onions, blackeyed peas, lemon juice and remaining stock. Simmer over very low heat for 1/2 to 3/4 hour.

Serve over steamed rice.

Serves 4 to 6

For the weekend of 27 January, 1927, when the great Arabian Nights festival was held at Opa-locka, Mrs. Frank S. Bush prepared what she called "cous-cous a la Opa-locka," which she described as "probably Irish lamb stew with a Moroccan accent." Her surviving children, Janet Hall, of Boynton Beach, and poet-historian Frank S. FitzGerald-Bush, author of A Dream of Araby: Glenn H. Curtiss and the Founding of Opa-locka," supplied their mother's recipe.

"One and a half lbs. lamb, cut into 1-inch squares
Two or three large onions, finely chopped
Two green peppers (or one green pepper and one red, for added color) finely chopped
Five or six stalks of celery, finely sliced
Three or four cups fresh green peas
Six or seven carrots, thinly sliced"

"Using a large, deep skillet (so that vegetables may be cooked in the same pot) sauté lamb in cooking oil (olive oil if one so chooses) until meat has just browned. Slowly add a cup or more of water, then add prepared vegetables, and further water, cooking until all is tender, then add seasonings, to taste (a touch of curry is good, as well as your favorite spices). Thicken the sauce or pot-liquor with a little corn-starch. Serve over a bowl of boiled rice. Boiled wheat is the traditional base for cous-cous, but difficult to find and even more difficult to cook."
– Lady Irene Bush

CROWN ROAST OF LAMB WITH CRANBERRY STUFFING

This gourmet recipe, a visual delight, comes to us from Pat's Captain's Table, Deerfield Beach, Florida.
The crown is made by joining two racks of lamb to form a circle and the center is stuffed with savory cranberry filling. The bones are often decorated with paper frills, but a small glazed onion on each bone tip make an unusual and edible garnish.

Crown roast of lamb, 16 ribs

1 cup beef drippings

CRANBERRY STUFFING

1 pound cranberries	1 clove garlic, peeled and crushed
1 cup chicken stock	1 pound mushrooms, chopped
2 tablespoons sugar	4 tablespoons parsley, chopped
2 tablespoons butter	1-1/2 teaspoons ground thyme
1 onion, finely chopped	2 cups fresh white bread crumbs

1 egg, lightly beaten

Salt and pepper, to taste

Glazed onions (garnish)

Preheat oven to 375 degrees.
Boil cranberries, stock and sugar until berries burst and liquid is reduced to a thick sauce.
In butter sauté the onion until soft. Add garlic and cook for 1 minute; add mushrooms. In a bowl, combine the cranberries and the onion-mushroom mixture with the parsley, thyme, and bread crumbs. Mix the egg thoroughly with stuffing. Season to taste.
Spoon stuffing into the hollow crown. Wrap foil around the bone tips to protect them. Roast on a low shelf for 10 minutes. Reduce heat to 350 degrees and continue roasting. Allow 15 to 16 minutes to the pound. Baste often with drippings.
Remove the roast and keep it warm. Skim off as much fat as possible; boil the pan juices and stir to make a gravy. Pour into a warm sauceboat.

Serves 6 to 8

SWEET AND SOUR HAM LOAF

3 pounds smoked ham, ground

3 pounds pork loin, ground

2 cups graham cracker crumbs

3/4 cup milk

4 eggs

2 small cans tomato paste

1-1/2 cups brown sugar

1/2 cup water

2/3 cup white vinegar

1-1/4 teaspoons dry mustard

Preheat oven to 325 degrees.

Thoroughly mix ham, pork, graham cracker crumbs, milk and eggs. Form mixture into a loaf.

Mix together tomato paste, brown sugar, water, vinegar and dry mustard. Spread on top of ham loaf.

Bake for 1 to 1-1/4 hours. Baste occasionally.

Serves 20

Note: This recipe can be halved.

A BEAUTIFUL DREAM
Opa-locka was founded in 1926 by pioneer aviator, inventor, and aircraft manufacturer Glenn H. Curtiss. Mr. Curtiss coined the name of his city from the first and last syllables of its Indian name "Opa-tishawauckalocka," and intended it to be the "most perfect city that planning and engineering could achieve, and the most beautiful that the art of man could conceive."

He chose New York architect Bernhardt E. Muller to design the buildings for the city, whose streets were laid out by Clinton McKenzie, designer of the street plans of Coral Gables and Miami Springs. The original idea of a medieval English village was abandoned in favor of an Arabian Nights theme, based on the One Thousand and One tales of the fabled Princess Scheherazade.

The Frank S. Bush family lived at "Pine Shadows," on Peri Street, where their Sunday evening "at homes" provided a center for Opa-locka's early social activities. Irene Bush, British-born and a great-granddaughter of Queen Victoria, served her guests scrambled eggs and Virginia ham at these weekly gatherings . . .

Sally Tommy's bead collection

SPIT-ROASTED HOLIDAY PORK

4 jars strained apricot baby food	1/8 teaspoon ground ginger
1/3 cup honey	1/8 teaspoon pepper
1/4 cup fresh lemon juice	Quilted broiling foil
1/4 cup soy sauce	
1/2 clove garlic, minced	
1 small onion, minced	
1 cup ginger ale	

5 pound pork roast, chine bone removed, tied for roasting

Marinate roast for 4 to 5 hours with 2 jars strained apricots, honey, lemon juice, soy sauce, garlic, onion, ginger ale, ginger and pepper. Turn occasionally.

Line charcoal grill with quilted foil. Let coals burn down until covered with gray ash. Remove pork from marinade, reserving marinade.

Place roast on spit and rotate over low coals for 3-1/2 hours or until done.

Roast should register 185 degrees on a meat thermometer when done. During the last 1/2 hour, baste frequently with marinade. During last 5 minutes, spread 1 jar of strained apricots over roast. Heat remaining marinade with 1 jar strained apricots and serve as a sauce with the meat.

GARNISH

1 can (1 pound 13 ounces) whole unpeeled apricots

1 tablespoon lemon rind, grated

1/4 cup coconut, freshly grated

Parsley sprigs

Heat apricots and lemon rind. Remove roast to a hot serving platter. Garnish with apricots sprinkled with coconut.

Serves 8 to 10

Note: If roasting in an oven, cook for 32 minutes per pound at 325 degrees.

CROWN ROAST OF PORK AND CHESTNUT STUFFING

Crown roast of pork

Salt and pepper, to taste

Pinch of nutmeg

1/2 to 1 cup white wine, heated

Butter for basting

3 tablespoons pan drippings

3 tablespoons flour

1-1/2 cups heavy cream

Preheat oven to 325 degrees.

Rub pork with salt, freshly ground pepper and nutmeg. Wrap bone ends in foil. Fill center with stuffing and top with butter.

Place pork on a rack in a baking pan. Roast 20 minutes per pound. Baste frequently with butter and white wine.

For gravy, heat 3 tablespoons pan drippings with 3 tablespoons flour. Add cream and stir until smooth. Season to taste.

Allow 2 ribs per person.

CHESTNUT STUFFING

1 cup onions, finely chopped

1/2 cup (1 stick) butter, melted

2 garlic cloves, finely chopped

2 teaspoons salt

1 teaspoon black pepper, freshly ground

1 teaspoon sage

2 cups bread crumbs

1 cup whole chestnuts, canned in brine, drained

1/4 cup parsley, chopped

1/2 cup Madeira or sherry

Sauté onions in butter until tender. Add garlic, salt, pepper and sage. Combine with bread crumbs, chestnuts and parsley. Add additional butter, if you like. Add Madeira or sherry.

"One of Aunty's stories was about a pig that attained all the immortality of the one that originated roast pork. Harvey's father use to drop Aunty's mail off as he went by, and that particular day preceding the pig adventure, he stopped long enough to say they were about to kill a pig and he invited her to come and eat sausage. Meat was so scarce and such a treat that, come morning, Aunty began to argue with herself as to whether he meant breakfast, dinner or supper. Finally to be on the safe side, she started up the road as soon as she had her morning coffee and fed the chickens.

"Others must have had the same doubts in their minds because when she arrived, early as it was, everyone else who had heard of it was already there. Way out to the road she could smell the sausage cooking.

"Harvey's mother and grandmother were manning the biscuit pans and someone was making coffee as fast as the pot was emptied. The neighbors had organized themselves and were taking turns at the handworking meat grinder and frying pans.

"It was like that famous 'From morn to noon from noon to dewey eve' affair. The party truly lasted until nightfall. Not a shred of that pig remained when the last guest – Aunty – departed, but it was a party that probably will live in all their memories on down the years."

– Annie Mayhue Fitzpatrick, from a regular column "Lest We Forget," printed in the Homestead Leader.

RENGES AFTER THE PORTUGALL FASHION

This splendid recipe comes from Delightes for Ladies, to adorne their Persons, Tables, closets, and distillatories *by Sir Hugh Platt, London, England, 1602.*

"Take Orenges & coare them on the side and lay them in water, then boile them in fair water til they be tender, shift them in the boyling to take away their bitternesse, then take sugar and boyle it to the height of sirup as much as will cover them, and so put your Orenges into it, and that will make them take sugar. If you have 24 Orenges, beate 8 of them till they come to paste with a pounde of fine sugar, then fill every one of the other Orenges with the same, and so boile them again in your sirup: then there will be marmelade of orenges within your orenges, & it wil cut like an hard egge."

SOUR ORANGE ROAST PORK

The sour orange was the only orange known to Europe for four hundred years. For a time the British imported it from Florida to use in their famous bitter orange marmalade.

2-1/2 to 4 pound pork loin, boneless

Preheat oven to 325 degrees.
    Marinate roast overnight. Cook 30 minutes per pound.

SOUR ORANGE MARINADE

1/4 cup soy sauce

2 cloves garlic, crushed

Juice of 2 sour oranges

Combine ingredients.

Serves 4 to 6

Note: Citrus fruit is not native to Florida. It was introduced by the Spaniards and it adapted readily to our soil and climate. It was cultivated by the Seminoles on the high ground of the Everglades hammocks. Remnants of those groves exist today.

PIONEER PIG PICKIN'

1 extra large smoked ham, fully cooked

Worcestershire sauce, for basting

Preheat oven to 250 degrees.

Place ham in a large pan. Baste every hour with Worcestershire sauce. Cook for 6 to 8 hours until crispy tender and it falls apart when done.

Serves 40

Coontie starch mill in pioneer Coconut Grove

JAMBALAYA WITH HAM AND SHRIMP

This scrumptious dish was a winner in the March of Dimes Gourmet Gala.

1/2 cup (1 stick) butter

3 cups onions, chopped

5 cloves garlic, chopped

1 can (28 ounces) Progresso tomatoes, crushed

6 ounces tomato paste

1 cup celery, chopped

1 cup green pepper, chopped

2 tablespoons parsley, chopped

1-1/2 teaspoons salt

1/2 teaspoon pepper

1/2 teaspoon cayenne pepper

1 teaspoon thyme

1/4 teaspoon cloves, ground

1-1/4 pound smoked ham, diced in 1/4-inch cubes

3 pounds shrimp, shelled, deveined and cooked

Melt butter in large heavy casserole. Cook onions and garlic until soft but not brown. Add tomatoes and paste and cook for 3 minutes. Add everything else except shrimp and ham. Cook uncovered until vegetables are done. May be held at this point until ready for use. Simmer gently, adding water if needed.

When ready to serve, add ham and heat for 5 minutes. Add shrimp and heat through. (Shrimp may be split lengthwise before adding to mixture).

Serve over rice.

Serves 6 to 8

INDONESIAN SKEWERED PORK SATES

"Sates" are sold from little carts at public gatherings in Indonesia like hot dogs are sold at American ball games. This recipe uses pork, but chicken, beef or veal are equally suitable.

1 large onion, minced

4 cloves garlic, minced or crushed

2 teaspoons pepper

3/4 cup lime juice

1 cup soy sauce

1/2 cup dark molasses

1 cup salad oil

5 pounds boneless lean pork, cut into 1-inch cubes.

Make sauce by combining onion, garlic, pepper, lime juice, soy sauce, molasses and salad oil. Whirl in a blender. Marinate meat for 3 to 4 hours.

Skewer meat on wet bamboo sticks, 3 or 4 pieces to each stick. Grill over charcoal until meat is brown and crisp on all sides, approximately 15 to 20 minutes. Do not overcook or the meat will be dry. Serve remaining marinade, heated, with the sates.

25 servings

TROPICAL SPARERIBS

1 cup soy sauce

1 cup Cointreau

1 cup honey

1 can (13-1/2 ounces) crushed pineapple, undrained

4 to 5 lemons, thinly sliced

1 tablespoons ginger, grated

8 cloves garlic, crushed

6 to 8 pounds spareribs

In a mixing bowl blend soy sauce, honey, Cointreau, pineapple, lemons, ginger and garlic.

Arrange spareribs in roasting pan, cover with marinade for 2 hours or overnight. Baste ribs with marinade while baking, broiling or grilling until done.

Serves 6 to 8

. . . .

VENISON STEAKS

Venison steaks, 1/2-inch thick

Salt and pepper, to taste

Butter, melted for basting

1/4 cup (1/2 stick) butter

2 tablespoons currant jelly

2 tablespoons parsley, minced

Salt and pepper, to taste

Steaks are cut from the loin and the upper leg. Sprinkle with salt and pepper, spread with melted butter and broil.

Put on a hot platter and spread with a mixture of butter, jelly, parsley, salt and pepper. Let stand in a hot oven for a few minutes.

HUNGARIAN VEAL PAPRIKASH

1 1/2 pounds stewing veal, cut into small cubes

Salt and pepper, to taste

4 tablespoons (1/2 stick) butter

1 large onion, finely chopped

2 tablespoons flour (2 tablespoons of sour cream may be substituted)

1 tablespoon paprika

1/2 cup white wine

Cover veal with water, adding salt and pepper. Simmer until veal is tender, approximately 1 hour. Remove any froth as the veal cooks. Drain veal and reserve stock.

Sauté onion and butter until onion is golden, not brown. Slowly stir in flour and paprika. Add 1 cup of reserved veal stock and wine. Stir until all lumps disappear.

Add the veal. Simmer 20 minutes. If sauce seems too thick, add more wine or stock.

Serve with rice or noodles.

Serves 4

BIG CYPRESS ROAST VENISON

5 to 6 pound venison roast

2 tablespoons bacon fat

Marinate venison in a glass dish. Cover and refrigerate for 2 days, turning often.

Remove meat from marinade and pat dry. Strain and reserve marinade.

In Dutch oven brown meat in fat on all sides. Add 1/2 cup marinade, cover and simmer over low heat for 2 to 3 hours or until tender. When needed, add small amounts of marinade.

Remove roast to hot serving dish and slice thickly. Keep hot. Make gravy with pan liquids. Pour gravy over meat. Serve with wild rice.

MARINADE

1 cup dry red wine

1 cup water

1-1/2 teaspoons salt

2 bay leaves

10 whole cloves

1 onion, chopped

2 chili peppers

5 whole allspice berries

Combine all ingredients.

Serves 6 to 8

OKEECHOBEE OPOSSUM

This pioneer recipe was published in 1938 in *The Southern Cookbook of Fine Old Recipes,* compiled and edited by Lillie S. Lustig, S. Claire Sondlhein and Sarah Rensel.

"The Opossum is a very fat animal, with a peculiarly flavored meat. It is dressed much as one would dress a suckling pig, removing the entrails, and if desired, the head and tail. After it has been dressed, wash thoroughly inside and outside with hot water. Cover with cold water to which has been added 1 cup of salt. Allow to stand overnight. In the morning, drain off the salted water and rinse well with clear, boiling water.

"Stuff the opossum . . . and roast in a moderate oven until the meat is very tender and richly browned."

Note: We could not find a Villager willing to catch a 'possum and test this recipe. You are on your own.

ZESTY LEMON ZUCCHINI

4 zucchini, peeled

Juice of 1 lemon

3 tablespoons butter, melted

Salt and lemon pepper, to taste

1/4 cup Parmesan cheese, grated

Preheat oven to 350 degrees.

Rake zucchini with a fork, cut lengthwise and place in a buttered casserole. Baste with lemon and remaining butter. Sprinkle with salt, lemon pepper and Parmesan cheese. Bake for 30 minutes or until golden brown.

Serves 4 to 8

. . . .

SAUTÉED GARLIC ZUCCHINI

1 1/2 pounds zucchini, unpeeled, scrubbed, shredded

6 tablespoons sweet butter

2 cloves of garlic, pressed

1/2 teaspoon salt, or to taste

Quickly sauté garlic and zucchini in butter, about 5 minutes. Add salt and serve.

Serves 6

VILLAGER BAKED VIDALIA ONIONS

1 large Vidalia onion per person, cored half-way down

2 beef or chicken bouillon cubes per onion

2 tablespoons brown sugar per onion

1 small ice cube per onion

Preheat oven to 350 degrees.

Put each onion in a small baking dish. Place bouillon cubes, brown sugar and ice cube in the center. Cover with foil and bake for 25 to 30 minutes.

One onion per person

. . . .

BROILED CURRIED TOMATOES

6 tomatoes, halved

3/4 cup onion, minced

1/4 teaspoon curry powder

1/4 teaspoon sugar

1/2 teaspoon salt

1/4 cup (1/2 stick) butter

2 tablespoons parsley, chopped (garnish)

Combine onion, curry powder, sugar and salt. Top each tomato half with a tablespoon of mixture and a teaspoon of butter. Broil under medium heat for 8 to 10 minutes. Sprinkle with parsley.

Serves 6

CAPONATA

Caponata is the Italian version of the French Ratatouille. It is excellent with cold roast meat.

1/2 cup olive oil

2 large onions, coarsely chopped

2 medium eggplants, unpeeled, chopped

1-1/2 cups celery, cut into 1-inch pieces

2 bell peppers, seeded, cut into 1-inch pieces

2 cloves garlic, peeled, finely chopped

2-1/2 pounds tomatoes, peeled and diced or 1 can (28 ounces) plum tomatoes

1/3 cup red wine vinegar

Salt and pepper, to taste

2 tablespoons sugar

1/4 cup fresh basil, chopped or 2 tablespoons dried basil

3 tablespoons tomato paste

1/2 cup parsley, chopped

1/4 cup green olives, sliced

Sauté onion, eggplant and celery. Add other ingredients and stir. Cover and simmer for 30 minutes. Remove lid and simmer for 10 more minutes. Chill.

Can be served hot, cold or at room temperature. Keeps in refrigerator for 2 weeks.

Serves 6 to 8

ROASTED SWISS ONIONS

2 large onions, sliced

5 tablespoons butter

6 hard-boiled eggs, sliced

3 tablespoons flour

1-1/2 cups milk, warmed

1/4 cup Swiss cheese, grated

Salt and pepper, to taste

Preheat oven to 350 degrees.
Thoroughly butter a 2-quart oblong baking dish.
Sauté onions in 2 tablespoons butter until soft. Place onions in baking dish, arrange egg slices on top.
In a saucepan over medium heat, melt 3 tablespoons butter. Add flour to make a roux. Cook about 3 minutes. Stir in milk until sauce thickens, add cheese and blend. Add salt and pepper.
Pour sauce over onions and eggs. Bake until light brown on top, about 5 minutes.

Serves 4 to 6

FRESH PEA OR CARROT PURÉE

1 1/2 cups fresh peas or sliced young carrots
4 tablespoons chicken stock
4 tablespoons (1/2 stick) butter
1 large potato, peeled, boiled and quartered
1 egg yolk, beaten
2 to 3 tablespoons heavy cream
1/2 teaspoon sugar, or to taste
Lemon juice, to taste
Salt and freshly ground pepper, to taste

Place vegetables, chicken stock and butter in a saucepan. Bring to a boil, cover with a sheet of waxed paper. Reduce heat to medium and simmer for 12 minutes.

Pour into food processor or blender. Add boiled potato. Blend on high speed for 2 minutes, scraping sides of bowl occasionally.

Return purée to saucepan. Beat vigorously with a wooden spoon over moderate heat until thoroughly heated, adding beaten egg yolk and enough cream so the purée holds its shape.

Season with sugar, a squeeze of lemon juice, salt and freshly ground pepper.

Serves 6

Note: Serve in a tomato shell or as a colorful garnish.

SPINACH PURÉE

2 packages (10 ounces each) frozen spinach, cooked, chopped and squeezed dry

1/2 cup (1 stick) butter

1/2 cup cottage cheese

3 tablespoons Parmesan cheese, grated

1/2 teaspoon nutmeg, freshly ground

1/2 teaspoon pepper, freshly ground

Pinch of salt

Preheat oven to 325 degrees.

While spinach is still warm, purée all ingredients in a blender. Pour into medium-size soufflé dish. Bake 20 minutes or just until heated.

This dish can be assembled ahead and cooked at serving time.

Serves 6

Storm-damaged bark at Coffin Patches

THE 1935 HURRICANE
"I remember when we had the warning of the hurricane of 1935. My father called and said, 'You'd better get home ... and get me some cigars.' I got to my father's house and we sat there and played gin rummy. Suddenly my father said, 'The wind has stopped,' and I didn't hear a thing. We just got the fringes. It was the Labor Day hurricane that hit the Keys.

"In 1907 my father began publishing the Miami Morning News-Record and it later became The Herald. He used to write editorials saying that you've got to have bridges as well as causeways. "This time the hurricane tides, wind and rain carried the water over the causeways. The tide was so high that the railroad cars were on their sides. The trains and people hadn't gotten out of the Keys quickly enough. It was not the water going over, but the water going back that killed them. Undertow is terrible." – Marjorie Stoneman Douglas

FIDDLE HEAD FERNS WITH SHALLOTS

The "fiddle head" are the coiled very young fronds, which resemble the head of a violin. Buy them at specialty vegetable stores or cut them from your own fern garden. Pioneer cooks used these native greens to add variety to their diets.

6 to 8 ounces fresh fiddle head fern tips, washed

6 shallots, finely chopped

2 tablespoons butter

2 tablespoons fresh dill, chopped

Salt and white pepper, to taste

Cook ferns in 1/2 cup boiling water for 3 to 5 minutes or until tender. Remove pan from heat.

Sauté shallots in butter. Add fern and dill. Season to taste.

Serves 6

• • • • • • • • • • • • • • • • • •

ALICE'S DEEP-DARK-SECRET BAKED BEANS

2 cans (14 ounces each) baked beans

1 pound hot sausage, sautéed and crumbled

Dash Worcestershire sauce

1 cup catsup

1 to 1-1/2 cups of coffee

Brown sugar, to taste

Preheat oven to 350 degrees.

Mix all ingredients, and bake for 1 hour.

Serves 8

LINGUINI WITH CLAM AND ARTICHOKE SAUCE

1/4 cup olive oil

4 tablespoons (1/2 stick) butter

1 teaspoon flour

1 cup chicken broth

3 to 4 cloves of garlic, crushed

1 tablespoon fresh parsley, minced

2 teaspoons fresh lemon juice

Salt and pepper, to taste

1 can (14 ounces) artichoke hearts, drained and quartered

1 can (10 ounces) whole baby clams, drained

2 to 3 tablespoons Parmesan cheese, finely grated

2 teaspoons small capers, drained

1/2 pound linguini

In a heavy skillet or 2-quart saucepan, heat olive oil and butter. Add flour and cook 3 minutes over medium heat, stirring often.

Stir in broth, reduce heat and cook 1 minute. Add garlic, parsley, lemon juice, salt and pepper. Cook over low heat about 5 minutes. Stir in artichokes, clams, cheese and capers. Continue cooking, stirring frequently for 10 minutes.

Meanwhile, cook linguini in rapidly boiling salted water until just "al dente," about 6 minutes. Drain and combine with clam and artichoke sauce.

Serves 3 to 4

WILD RICE WITH MUSHROOMS AND MARJORAM

1/2 cup wild rice

1-1/2 cups chicken broth

1 tablespoon butter

2 tablespoons onion, chopped

1 tablespoon green pepper, chopped

4 ounces mushrooms, chopped

1/2 can (10-1/2 ounces) condensed cream of mushroom soup

1/2 cup heavy cream

1 teaspoon marjoram

Dash dried basil

Dash tarragon

1/4 teaspoon each curry, salt and fresh ground pepper

Wash rice well. Cook in broth following package directions.

Sauté onions, green peppers and mushrooms in butter 5 minutes. Stir in soup, cream and herbs. Add to rice, stirring occasionally. Keep warm until ready to serve.

Serves 6

Note: Serve with Tarragon Cornish Game Hens. (See Index.)

CHEESE PUFF CASSEROLE

1 cup flour

1/2 teaspoon each salt and pepper

1-1/2 cups sour cream

1/4 cup Parmesan cheese, grated

5 eggs, separated

1 tablespoon Parmesan cheese, grated

Preheat oven to 350 degrees.

Thoroughly grease 1-1/2 quart casserole dish.

Set casserole in a baking pan and place in oven. Pour 1 inch of boiling water around casserole. Let casserole heat while preparing cheese puff.

Combine flour, salt and pepper in a mixing bowl. Thoroughly blend in sour cream and 1/4 cup cheese. Add unbeaten egg yolks, beating until ivory colored. Beat egg whites until stiff, but not dry. Gently fold into sour cream mixture.

Pour into hot casserole. Sprinkle with 1 tablespoon of Parmesan cheese. Bake about 1 hour, until puffy and delicately browned and a knife blade inserted between center and outside edge comes out clean.

Serve immediately with melted butter and additional fresh Parmesan cheese.

Serves 6

UNT BELLA'S DREAM
Isabella (Aunt Bella) Peacock
was determined that the children of Coconut Grove have a Sunday School so they could learn the Bible. As the wife of the owner of Bayview House, the Biscayne Bay area's first mainland hotel, she solicited contributions from guests and the skippers of boats moored in the Bay to raise money to achieve her goal.

In 1887, when enough money had been collected, she donated some of her family property and encouraged the local men to build a sturdy little one-room schoolhouse out of lumber retrieved from a shipwreck.

It may have been "Aunt Bella's dream" but it was young Charley Frow's father, Joseph, who walked 79 hot and sandy miles up the beach to Lake Worth to register the ten children necessary for a school. He included the name of his youngest child, not yet 6, to the roll so the requirement of 10 children could be met.

The "Sunday School" became the educational, religious and social center for the enterprising bayfront community of 30 people.

Nearly a century later the restored schoolhouse, Dade County's first, has been moved to the beautiful grounds of Coconut Grove's Plymouth Congregational Church. It stands there as a monument to the early Grove families and their dedication to education. The tiny schoolhouse celebrates its centennial in 1987.

SPRING VEGETABLES

12 small red new potatoes

6 to 8 large lettuce leaves

1 pound very small carrots, peeled

12 small white onions, peeled

2 sprigs parsley

1/2 cup boiling water

2 teaspoons sugar

Salt and pepper, to taste

1/2 cup (1 stick) butter, melted

2 packages (10 ounces each) frozen tiny peas

Pare 1/2-inch wide strip of skin around center of each potato.

Completely line bottom of large heavy skillet with 3 to 4 lettuce leaves. Add potatoes, carrots, onions and parsley. Pour on boiling water and sprinkle with seasonings. Add 1/3 cup of the butter and top with remaining lettuce leaves.

Cook over medium heat, tightly covered for 15 minutes. Separate frozen peas and add to skillet. Cover again and cook for 10 to 15 minutes or until all vegetables are tender.

To serve, discard parsley and lettuce. Spoon vegetables into a heated serving dish. Pour remaining butter over vegetables.

Serves 6

CUBAN BLACK BEANS

1 pound black beans

1 whole onion

1 green pepper, seeded and cut into strips

1 clove garlic, whole

4 cachucha peppers*

1 onion, chopped

1 green pepper, chopped

1 clove garlic, minced

1 bay leaf

1/2 teaspoon oregano

Salt, to taste

1 tablespoon vinegar

1/4 cup olive oil

1/4 cup red wine

Cover beans with 5 cups of water and soak overnight, drain. In 5 cups water, simmer beans, whole onion, garlic, pepper strips and cachucha pepper. Cook until tender.

Sauté chopped onion, chopped peppers and minced garlic in small amount of oil until tender. Add to beans. Add bay leaf, oregano and salt. Continue cooking for 2 to 3 hours over low heat.

Before serving add vinegar, olive oil and red wine. Stir well and serve over rice.

Serves 8 to 10

*Cachucha peppers are shaped like flat red or green rosettes. Seldom sold canned, they may be found fresh in Latin markets. The flavor is milder than jalapeño peppers; however, as with all peppers, use them cautiously.

P an American Airways was established by young Juan Trippe in 1927. He saw South Florida as "The Gateway to South America." The first flights carried 722 pounds of mail between Key West and Havana, Cuba, 90 miles away.

Soon after, Pan American Field was built at Le Jeune Road and 36th Street. It evolved into Miami International Airport.

But the most interesting airport was opened at Dinner Key for the island-hopping amphibious airplanes. When a seaplane would gently splash down in the channel after a trip to Nassau or Bimini, divers would swim out and attach wheels to the pontoons. Tractors could then haul the planes ashore.

President Franklin Roosevelt boarded one of the famous Pan Am Clippers at Dinner Key when he was on his way to meet Winston Churchill in Casablanca.

Dinner Key has its own story. Early residents on a sailing trip from Snapper Creek or Cutler to the Miami River or Lemon City found it a convenient stopping place for a meal. It was a military base during World War I and a naval and Coast Guard base in World War II. Today, Miami City Hall occupies the original waterfront Pan American terminal building.

A first-hand account of the 1926 hurricane, written by Mrs. Kenneth Ashby, who lived in the E.R. Thomas House on the ocean at 40th Street and Collins Avenue on Miami Beach..."My son-in-law, Eddie Brelsford, came for mother and me Friday evening and took us to their home, because we were so close to the ocean and alone. The weather bureau told us the storm was approaching but nothing alarming. I had plenty of time to have saved many things had the warnings warranted, but did not deem it necessary and saved nothing and our cottage, 'Seaweed' is utterly demolished. When the hurricane hit we were up all night trying to stop broken windows with mattresses, moving heavy furniture against those mattresses to try and hold them against the flood but finally there was nothing to do but take the elements. We had our canned food, no bread, no ice, heads aching for lack of hot coffee, nerves gone and stomachs sick as a consequence. That night I slept on Alice's fur coat on the dining table."

Note: Had the two women remained in the cottage, no doubt they would have gone the way of their belongings, never to be seen again. One exception was a small mahogany table, still in use, which was found several miles away on the Miami Beach Golf Course.

FLAGEOLET BEANS IN CREAM

Flageolets, French beans, dried and shelled, are sometimes called chick peas or garbanzos.

1 pound dried flageolet beans

8 cups cold water

1 carrot

1 large onion stuck with 4 cloves

2 ribs celery, trimmed

3 sprigs fresh parsley

1 bay leaf

1/4 teaspoon dried thyme

Salt and freshly ground pepper, to taste

2 tablespoons butter

1 teaspoon garlic, finely minced

1 tablespoon shallots, finely chopped

1/2 cup parsley, chopped

1 cup heavy cream

Soak beans overnight in enough water to cover plus about 2 inches. Drain beans, add 8 cups of cold water, the carrot and the onion stuck with cloves. Tie a bouquet garni of celery, parsley sprigs and bay leaf. Add salt, pepper and thyme. Bring to a boil. Simmer covered for 2 hours or until tender. Discard bouquet garni. Remove carrot and cut into small cubes.

Drain beans, reserving 1/2 cup of cooking liquid. Set aside. Heat the butter in a large skillet and add garlic and shallots. Cook briefly, add beans, parsley, carrot, reserved cooking liquid and cream. Simmer 5 minutes and serve.

Serves 8 to 10

Note: We recommend serving these with French Country Leg of Lamb. (See Index.)

RICOTTA GNOCCHI WITH PESTO GENOVESE

2 eggs	
1 pound Ricotta cheese	
1/2 cup Parmesan cheese, freshly grated	
3 to 4 cups flour	

Beat eggs. Add Ricotta cheese and when well mixed stir in grated Parmesan. Work in 3 to 4 cups of flour until dough can be rolled. Knead dough until smooth.

Cut into 2-inch wide pieces. Roll into sticks about 1-inch in diameter. Slice into 1-inch pieces. Place on floured surface to prevent sticking. Press each piece against the concave surface of a fork to give a ridged pattern.

Cook gnocchi in a large pan of boiling salted water approximately 5 minutes; drain.

PESTO GENOVESE SAUCE

6 sprigs parsley	3 tablespoons olive oil
3 sprigs marjoram	2 tablespoons butter, softened
1/2 cup pine nuts	1/4 teaspoon salt
3 cloves garlic, crushed	Pepper, to taste
1/3 cup Parmesan cheese, grated	
1/3 cup Romano cheese, grated	
1 cup fresh basil leaves, washed and dried	
4 spinach leaves, washed and dried	

Put basil, spinach, parsley, marjoram, pine nuts and garlic in a food processor with steel blade or in a blender and chop. With motor running, slowly add olive oil and butter.

Shut off the motor and add cheeses, salt and pepper. Process again until smooth and pour over hot gnocchi.

Makes 1 cup
Serves 4

Note: Omit the cheeses and increase the amount of pine nuts to 3/4 cup for a sauce that is delicious over hot or cold poached fish.

CORAL GABLES HOUSE
In 1898, Solomon Merrick, a New England minister, moved to South Florida to join former parishioners who were living in the warmth of a little-known place, Cocoanut Grove, on the shore of Biscayne Bay. He bought land sight unseen and brought his young son George to Florida to see the family's new homestead.

The 160 acre tract was called "Guavonia" for the wild guavas growing there. He got quite a surprise when he found it was four miles from the "civilization" of Cocoanut Grove. A lot of work would be necessary to clear the land for growing citrus and vegetables. The work became easier with the arrival of the rest of the family and his wife, Althea, who drew up the plans for a coral rock house.

Because the land was on a flood plain and could be under as much as four feet of water in the rainy season, the house was built high off the ground. This had the added advantage of having the living areas readily accessible to the slightest breeze. A wide and gracious porch sheltering it on the south and west and very thick walls effectively kept the interior cool in steamy subtropical summers.

The roof was high and gabled and covered with colorful Ludovici tiles from Georgia, which gave the home its name, Coral Gables House. It is now open to the public as a museum.

TARPON SPRINGS PASTITSIO

There is a Greek community north of Tampa called Tarpon Springs. The natives of this charming town came from Greece many years ago to harvest sponges from the Gulf of Mexico.

1 pound macaroni

1 pound (4 sticks) butter, melted

1 cup Mezithra cheese, if available

1/2 cup each Romano and Parmesan cheese, grated

1 cup Feta cheese, crumbled

5 eggs, slightly beaten

2 cups milk

8 phyllo pastry sheets

Salt and pepper, to taste

Preheat oven to 350 degrees.

Brush a 9 x 13-inch baking dish with some melted butter.

Cook macaroni until tender and drain well. Mix macaroni with half of the melted butter in a large bowl Add cheeses, blend in eggs, milk, salt and pepper. Arrange in a baking dish.

Cover with phyllo, brushing each sheet with remaining butter. Score last 3 sheets with a sharp knife. Bake for 15 minutes. Reduce heat to 300 degrees and bake 30 minutes. Let cool for about 15 minutes and cut into squares.

Serves 12

Note: Great with leg of lamb or roast beef.

RISOTTO ALLA MILANESE
(Braised Rice with Saffron)

7 cups chicken stock

4 tablespoons (1/2 stick) butter

1/2 cup onions, finely chopped

2 cups long grain rice

1/2 cup white wine

1/8 teaspoon saffron, powdered or crushed threads

4 tablespoons (1/2 stick) butter

1/2 cup Parmesan cheese, grated

Heat chicken stock in 3 quart saucepan; keep barely simmering over low heat. In a deep sauté pan, sauté onions in 4 tablespoons butter until tender; do not let them brown. Add the rice and sauté until it takes on color and becomes somewhat opaque. Pour in the wine and boil until it is almost absorbed. Add 2 cups simmering stock to the rice. Cook uncovered, stirring occassionally, until liquid is almost absorbed. Stir in 2 more cups stock, continue stirring.

Steep saffron for a few minutes in 2 cups of the remaining stock. Pour over rice and cook until the stock is completely absorbed. Rice should be tender. If it is still firm, add the remaining stock 1/2 cup at a time. Continue cooking and stirring until the rice is soft, but not dried out.

Stir in the melted butter and grated cheese and serve at once.

Serves 6 to 8

Note: This is superb served with Osso Buco. (See Index.)

HE COMMON COONTIE PLANT

We know it as "arrowroot," but Florida pioneers called it either coontie, or cumpty. To the first settlers it meant hard work, a little cash in the pocket or a useful product for barter.

Thelma Peters, author of Lemon City, told us these facts: "Of the approximately thirty-five adult males at Biscayne Bay in 1880, more than half made starch. The primitive palm-like coontie plants were everywhere in the pine woods and seemed inexhaustible. A man could dig five or six barrels of roots a day, and nine barrels of roots would yield one barrel of starch worth nine dollars in Key West.

"Starch was a dependable source of cash for bay settlers until about 1900 when production began to move from the back yard to commercial mills. Most of the early mills were makeshift. A grinder could be made by driving rows of shoe peg nails into two short round logs and making one log turn against the other so that the nails chewed up the roots.

"One man ordered an apple mill from a mail catalog and others used cane grinders operated by horsepower."

Thelma Peters paused here to note that she would not include the complete process as it could be dangerous (if improperly done). Incompletely processed coontie roots and even the run-off water from frequent washings were poisonous to man and beast.

The crop could not be domesticated and in the 1940's real estate development paved over the few remaining woodland sources.

SEMINOLE SOFKEE

This recipe is from *The Pioneer Cook*, Boca Raton Historical Society.

1 cup grits

6 cups water

1 pound meat, cubed (the Seminoles used venison)

Vegetables (okra is a good choice)

1/4 cup water (optional)

1 tablespoon arrowroot (optional)

"Simmer grits in 6 cups of water with about a pound of meat. Add vegetables about a half hour before the meat is completely done. If the stew becomes too thick add more water. If the stew is not thick enough add a quarter cup of water mixed with tablespoon of arrowroot or corn starch. The finished stew should have a milky appearance."

Serves 6 to 8

Saluting the arrowroot starch industry. (Romer Collection)

JOHN PENNEKAMP'S GRITS SOUFFLÉ

1 cup coarse-grain grits (not instant)

4 cups water

1/2 cup onion, chopped

1 teaspoon salt

1/2 cup (1 stick) butter

2 cloves garlic, crushed

1/2 pound Velveeta cheese, cubed

1 pound sharp Cheddar cheese, shredded

4 eggs, beaten

Milk, enough when added to eggs to make 1 cup

1/4 cup (1/2 stick) butter, melted

2 small packages corn flakes, crushed

Preheat oven to 350 degrees.

Butter a casserole dish.

Cook grits with onions and salt according to package directions.

Combine 1/2 cup butter, garlic, cheeses, eggs and milk. Thoroughly stir into hot grits, pour into casserole. Sprinkle with corn flakes mixed with 1/4 cup butter.

Bake for 30 minutes.

Serves 4 to 6

SOUFFLÉ OLÉ

6 eggs, separated

1 tablespoon flour

1/4 teaspoon salt

1/4 teaspoon pepper

4 ounces fresh green chilies, seeded and roasted

1/2 pound Monterey Jack cheese, sliced

Preheat oven to 350 degrees.

Butter 7 x 13-inch baking dish.

Beat egg whites until stiff. Mix flour, salt and pepper with egg yolks. Beat until thoroughly mixed. Fold whites into yolk mix.

Pour half the mixture into baking dish. Spread chilies over the batter, cover with cheese slices. Add remaining batter.

Bake for 25 minutes.

Cut into squares and serve with Mexican *salsa picante.*

Serves 4

ANGEL HAIR PASTA WITH ROQUEFORT SAUCE

1 pound capellini (angel hair pasta), preferably spinach flavored

10 to 12 ounces Roquefort cheese, crumbled

2 cloves garlic, minced

1/2 cup (1 stick) butter

1 cup light cream

Pepper, to taste

2 carrots, sliced, steamed, and buttered

1/4 cup pistachio nuts, chopped

Boil and drain pasta and set aside.

In a saucepan melt Roquefort cheese in butter with garlic. Add cream and a dash of pepper. When mixture bubbles, remove from heat, pour over pasta. Add carrots and pistachio nuts and toss.

Serves 6 to 8

AFTER-DINNER DELIGHTS

CALAMONDIN FREEZE

1 cup all-purpose flour

1/4 cup brown sugar

1/2 cup walnuts, chopped

1/2 cup (1 stick) butter, melted

2 eggs, separated

1 can (14 ounces) sweetened condensed milk

1/2 cup fresh calamondin juice

1 teaspoon calamondin peel, grated

1/4 cup granulated sugar

Preheat oven to 350 degrees.

Combine flour, sugar and walnuts. Pour in butter and mix until crumbly. Bake for 20 minutes on cookie sheet, stirring occasionally, until crisp and golden brown. Cool.

Beat egg yolks until thick. Add milk, calamondin juice and grated peel. Stir until mixture thickens.

Beat egg whites until soft peaks form. Gradually add 1/4 cup sugar and beat until stiff peaks form. Fold egg whites into calamondin mixture until well blended.

Spread 2/3 of the crumb mixture on bottom of 8-inch square serving dish. Pour calamondin mixture on top. Sprinkle remaining crumbs on top. Cover with aluminum foil and freeze overnight.

Serves 6 to 8

MRS. PETERSON'S CRESCENT COOKIES

4 cups flour

1 cup (2 sticks) butter

4 egg yolks, beaten

1 cup sour cream

Work flour and butter together with the tips of your fingers, until it resembles corn meal. Add yolks and sour cream. Roll the size of walnuts. Place on large cookie sheet. Cover with foil and refrigerate overnight.

FILLING

2 cups walnuts, ground

1 cup sugar

4 egg whites, unbeaten

1 teaspoon vanilla

Juice of 1 small lemon

Preheat oven to 375 degrees.

Combine all ingredients.

Roll cookies on floured board and fill each cookie with 2/3 teaspoon filling. Roll and shape into crescents. Place on ungreased cookie sheet and bake for 20 minutes. Sprinkle with powdered sugar while still warm.

Makes 8 to 10 dozen

STRAWBERRY CRUNCH SOUFFLÉ SQUARES

CRUNCH TOPPING

1 cup all-purpose flour

1/2 cup (1 stick) butter, melted

1/2 cup brown sugar

1/2 cup walnuts, chopped

Preheat oven to 350 degrees.

Mix all ingredients and spread on 9 x 12-inch pan. Bake for 20 minutes. Stir occasionally to brown evenly. Spread 2/3 cooked crunch on bottom of pan. Reserve 1/3 for topping.

FILLING

1 pint strawberries, puréed

2 egg whites

2 tablespoons lemon juice

2/3 cup granulated sugar

1 pint heavy cream, whipped

Mix all ingredients except the cream at high speed until the mixture stands in peaks, about 10 minutes. Fold in whipped cream. Pour into pan over crumbs and top with remaining crumbs. Freeze 6 hours or overnight. Can be frozen for several months.

Cut into squares and serve at room temperature. Top with more whipped cream and fresh berries.

Makes 30 to 36 squares

CHOCOLATE MOUSSE LOAF

1-1/2 cups walnuts, finely chopped

12 ounces semisweet chocolate bits

3/4 cup (1-1/2 sticks) salted butter

3 tablespoons cocoa powder

1/3 cup sugar

4 egg yolks

5 egg whites

Pinch of salt

Generously butter bottom and sides of 1 quart glass loaf pan. Line bottom with parchment paper. Butter paper. Sprinkle 1 cup of walnuts over bottom and 2 inches up sides of pan, pressing into place. Set aside.

Combine chocolate, butter and cocoa in heavy saucepan and cook over low heat, stirring occasionally until chocolate and butter are melted. Remove from heat. Set pan in bowl of ice water to cool. Do not let chocolate harden. Transfer it to the large bowl of an electric mixer. Add sugar and beat at medium speed until well mixed. Beat in yolks, one at a time.

Beat the egg whites and salt in another large bowl until whites are stiff and glossy.

Stir 1/4 of the egg whites into chocolate mixture until well blended. Gently fold in remaining egg whites. Turn into prepared pan.

Cover with plastic wrap and refrigerate until well chilled. Carefully separate mousse from pan using thin sharp knife or a spatula. Invert mousse onto serving platter. Press remaining 1/2 cup of walnuts into mousse.

Serves 8 to 10

Note: If wrapped air tight, this mousse can be prepared up to 1 month ahead and frozen. Let thaw 24 hours in the refrigerator before serving.

CHOCOLATE TRUFFLES

7 ounces semisweet chocolate

1/2 cup whipping cream

2 tablespoons butter

3/4 cup powdered sugar, measured, then sifted

2 egg yolks

1 to 2 tablespoons orange liqueur

One of the following: unsweetened cocoa, coarsely chopped nuts or powdered sugar

Combine chocolate, cream and butter in top of a double boiler over simmering water. Add sugar and yolks and whisk until smooth. Remove from heat and add liqueur to taste. Place in a flat glass dish and chill until malleable (2 hours in the refrigerator or 1 hour in the freezer.)

Shape into small balls about the size of large olives. Roll in your choice of the last ingredients. Place in paper candy cups and refrigerate until hardened.

Makes 2 to 3 dozen

OLD-FASHIONED CARAMELS

2 cups sugar

2 cups light corn syrup

2 cups heavy cream

3/4 cup (1/2 can) evaporated milk

1/2 teaspoon salt

1/2 cup (1 stick) butter, cut up

1 tablespoon vanilla

Using a 10-inch diameter heavy aluminum pan with 6 to 8-inch high sides, cook all ingredients except butter to 235 degrees on a candy thermometer. Stir carefully and methodically to prevent sticking and burning. Add the butter and cook, stirring constantly, to 240 degrees. Remove from heat at EXACTLY 240 degrees. Add 1 tablespoon vanilla and stir.

Cool and cut into 1-inch squares; wrap individually and chill. Store in refrigerator to delay sugaring.

Makes about 2 pounds

Note: For chocolate caramels add 4-1/2 ounces unsweetened chocolate, previously shaved or cut fine. Mix and pour promptly into a square pan, about 3/4-inch deep.

CANDIED ORANGE PEEL

Peel from 6 large oranges

1 tablespoon salt

4 cups water

3 cups sugar

Hot water

Cover peel with salt water overnight. Drain and wash peel thoroughly. Cover peel with cold water and bring to a boil, repeat this 3 times, changing water each time.

Cut peel in 1/4-inch strips with scissors and place in saucepan. Add sugar and hot water, just enough to cover. Cook slowly until peel is translucent.

Drain, roll in granulated sugar and let dry. Store in air tight container.

Note: Use as a candy or in your favorite fruit cake or bread recipe. It is also delicious dipped in melted semisweet chocolate. Dry on cake rack over wax paper.

SYLLABUB

Syllabub is a frothy drink or dessert. In this country it dates back to Colonial times. The origin of the name is unknown; it may derive from the English word "silly" meaning "happy" and "bub" meaning a bubbling drink. Also called "silly bubbles."

1 lemon, juice and zest

1/2 cup sherry

2 tablespoons Cognac

1/2 cup sugar

1 cup heavy cream, chilled

1/8 teaspoon nutmeg, freshly grated

The day before, grate the zest of the lemon, reserving 1 tablespoon for garnish. Combine lemon juice with zest. Add sherry and Cognac and let rest overnight.

The next day, transfer lemon juice to 3 quart bowl, add sugar and stir until dissolved. Add cream and nutmeg, stirring continuously. Beat vigorously for 5 minutes with whisk until it holds soft peaks. Spoon it into a 2 or 3 ounce champagne glass. Add lemon zest and serve cool, but not chilled.

Serves 6

TRUMAN CAPOTE'S COLD BANANA PUDDING

3-3/4 cups milk

2 packages (3-1/4 ounces) vanilla pudding and pie mix

3 eggs, separated

1 cup heavy cream, stiffly beaten

2 teaspoons vanilla extract

1 package (3 ounces) ladyfingers

4 bananas, thinly sliced crosswise

1/8 teaspoon nutmeg

1/3 cup superfine sugar

In a medium saucepan, gradually blend milk with vanilla pudding and pie mix. Separate 3 eggs, adding yolks to pudding mixture and reserving whites for later use. Beat pudding mixture with electric or rotary beater until smooth.

Cook, stirring constantly, until pudding comes to a full boil. Remove from heat. Cover surface with foil or plastic wrap and cool for 20 to 30 minutes.

Fold in whipped cream and 2 teaspoons vanilla extract.

Preheat oven to 350 degrees.

Arrange half of the ladyfingers on the bottom of a 2-1/2 quart casserole or baking dish. Spoon half the pudding over the ladyfingers and arrange 2 sliced bananas on top. Repeat layers, sprinkling nutmeg on top of the final banana layer.

Beat the egg whites until foamy. Gradually add sugar, beating well until meringue is stiff. Spoon over pudding. Bake 7 to 8 minutes at 350 degrees or until meringue is lightly browned.

Serves 6 to 8

OLD-TIME BREAD PUDDING WITH BUTTERSCOTCH SAUCE

2 cups milk, scalded

1/4 cup (1/2 stick) butter

3 eggs

1/2 cup sugar

1/4 teaspoon salt

1 teaspoon cinnamon

3 cups bread cubes

1/2 cup raisins (optional)

Preheat oven to 350 degrees.

Scald milk and add butter. Beat eggs slightly and stir into milk mixture. Add sugar, salt and cinnamon.

Place bread and raisins in a 1-1/2 quart casserole. Pour milk mixture over bread and stir slightly to moisten.

Place casserole in a pan of warm water and bake for 40 to 45 minutes. Serve with butterscotch sauce.

BUTTERSCOTCH SAUCE

3/4 cup water

1 to 2 tablespoons cornstarch

3/4 cup brown sugar

2 tablespoons butter

Mix 1 to 2 tablespoons of the cold water with cornstarch. Heat sugar and water to boiling. Add cornstarch mixture to thicken slightly. Add butter and pour over pudding.

Serves 6

1

898

By the first decade of this century, Miami had turned into "Hometown U.S.A." It was a rocking chair town, the quiet streets lined with comfortable frame houses complete with broad porches. Everyone knew everybody else, at least by reputation. The hotels and the railroad were the primary businesses but there were many others ... dry goods, hardware, livery stables, trading posts. The hotels were seasonal, and the social season coincided with their opening and closing. The ladies of the community were involved with church, school and cultural activities; there were two moving picture houses and rounds of picnics and boating parties.

There were differences from other hometowns, of course. Indians still came down the river in their canoes to trade egret feathers and furs, you could still hear an occasional panther scream at night, and the Bay was a never-ending challenge to the young people. It was also the chief livelihood of many.

Soldiers were stationed here during the Spanish-American War. It was a rather unhappy experience on both sides. Miamians were not pleased with large numbers of bored and drunken soldiers. The soldiers themselves were mostly uneducated farm boys ready to fight but stuck in a dull backwater in the summertime with nothing to do. To make it worse, they had to wear government issue wool uniforms! Strange things happen to servicemen sent to Miami. The very soldiers who complained about the heat and isolation began to drift back in later years, bringing with them their families and dreams.

OLD WORLD ENGLISH TRIFLE WITH CRÈME ANGLAISE

ENGLISH TRIFLE

9-inch round sponge cake, cut across in 3 pieces

1/2 cup cream sherry

1 cup apricot, raspberry or strawberry jam

1 pint strawberries, blueberries, peaches or raspberries

Crème Anglaise, cooled

1 cup heavy cream, whipped with 2 tablespoons confectioners' sugar

1/2 cup slivered almonds, toasted

Put 1 layer of sponge cake in 9-inch crystal bowl. Sprinkle with sherry, using just enough to dampen cake. Cover with a layer of jam and spread with fruit. Pour 1/3 of the Crème Anglaise over fruit. Repeat twice. Chill for several hours. Decorate with whipped cream, fruit and almonds.

CRÈME ANGLAISE

5 egg yolks

6 tablespoons sugar

Pinch of salt

2 cups heavy cream

1 teaspoon vanilla

Combine egg yolks, sugar and salt in mixing bowl. Blend well with whisk. Scald heavy cream. Pour slowly into egg mixture.

Transfer mixture to a heavy saucepan and cook over low heat, stirring constantly with wooden spoon until mixture thinly coats spoon. Cool and add vanilla.

Serves 10 to 12

Note: Trifle may also be topped with meringue. Whip 3 egg whites with 5 tablespoons of sugar. Top Trifle with meringue and brown in a 350 degree oven. Be sure to use an ovenproof bowl.

SEVDA'S "TURKISH" BAKLAVA

SYRUP

2 cups granulated sugar

1 3/4 cups cold water

1 tablespoon lemon juice

In a saucepan mix all ingredients. Boil on medium heat for 20 minutes. Remove and let cool.

BAKLAVA

12 ounces walnuts, finely chopped

2 tablespoons sugar

1/4 teaspoon cinnamon

1 pound phyllo pastry

3/4 pound (3 sticks) sweet butter, clarified* and cooled

Preheat oven to 350 degrees. Grease a 9 x 13-inch pan.

Fold phyllo sheet in half in the pan, brush with butter. Repeat using 1/2 pound butter and half the phyllo dough.

Combine walnuts, sugar and cinnamon and spread on top of dough.

Continue placing phyllo sheets on walnut mixture, buttering each until remainder is used. Cut in diagonal squares almost to the bottom of the pan. Bake for 30 minutes in the middle of the oven. If not crispy after 30 minutes, continue baking a few more minutes at 325 degrees. Remove and cool for 30 minutes.

Spoon syrup mixture over pastry. Wait until syrup soaks in then add more syrup until all is used. Let sit at least 2 hours.

Serves 24

*To clarify butter, melt slowly. Allow milk solids to sink. Slowly pour clear liquid through a paper towel-lined sieve.

"I knew Mrs. Charles Deering very well. I used to go down there for lunch and dinner and you'd have cocktails perhaps in the library, and then you'd go through the house and along the boardway to the old house. You'd have dinner there in what was a great dining room with a big old fashioned kitchen. Then you'd come back to the living room of the other house and have coffee there and spend the evening. It made a wonderful place for entertaining."
– Marjorie Stoneman Douglas

SANTA MARIA TOFFEE MERINGUE

6 egg whites

1/2 teaspoon cream of tartar

Pinch of salt 1-1/2 cups sugar

1 pint whipping cream, whipped with 1 teaspoon vanilla

5 to 6 Heath bars, frozen and crushed

Preheat oven to 300 degrees.

Line two 11 x 15-inch pans with foil.

Beat egg whites, cream of tartar and salt at the highest speed on mixer. Add sugar 1 tablespoon at a time, beating well after each addition. Beat until very stiff.

Pour meringue into pans, making sure to spread it into the corners. Bake 1 hour. Allow to cool.

Crush Heath bars or any frozen crispy candy.

When meringue is cool, remove from pans by inverting over platter. Peel off foil gently, taking care not to break meringue.

Place meringue on platter. Spread with half of the crushed candy and whipped cream flavored with vanilla. Repeat with the second layer. Place in the refrigerator overnight. Cut into small squares. This recipe is very rich and will melt in your mouth.

This can be frozen, but let it thaw before cutting.

Makes 4 dozen

COEUR À LA CRÈME AND STRAWBERRIES

Celebrate Valentine's Day with this lovely dessert.

1/3 cup cottage cheese, pressed through sieve

8 ounces cream cheese, room temperature

Pinch of salt

1 cup whipping cream

2 tablespoons vanilla

4 tablespoons powdered sugar

1 quart heart-shaped mold, lined with dampened cheesecloth large enough to allow a 2-inch overhang

Blend cottage cheese, cream cheese and salt. When fluffy, add vanilla and sugar.

Gradually add whipping cream, beating until the mixture is smooth. Pour into mold. Smooth top and cover with overhanging cheesecloth. Place mold on wire rack, set over pie plate and refrigerate at least 6 hours or overnight.

Unmold onto chilled platter and surround with strawberries.

Serves 6 to 8

MOCHA AMARETTO MOUSSE

6 ounces semisweet chocolate morsels

3 tablespoons apricot nectar

2 tablespoons Amaretto liqueur

2 eggs plus 2 egg yolks

1-1/2 tablespoons instant coffee crystals

1/4 cup sugar

1/2 teaspoon vanilla extract

3/4 teaspoon almond extract

1 cup heavy cream

Using a heavy bottomed pan or double boiler, melt chocolate, add apricot nectar and Amaretto. Stir constantly until the chocolate melts. Cool.

In blender, combine eggs, egg yolks, instant coffee, sugar, vanilla, and almond extracts. Add heavy cream; blend well. Add melted, cooled chocolate and blend until smooth.

Pour into bowl, 8 individual mousse glasses or custard cups. Cover and refrigerate several hours or overnight. This freezes well but do not garnish before freezing.

GARNISH

1 cup heavy cream

2 tablespoons powdered sugar

Dash of Amaretto liqueur and almond extract

Shaved chocolate curls

Before serving, whip cream and sugar. Add Amaretto liqueur and almond extract and whip to form stiff peaks. Swirl mixture on top of each mousse and sprinkle with shaved chocolate.

Serves 8

TORTONI CRÈME DE COCOA

2 egg whites

1/8 teaspoon cream of tartar

Dash of salt

1 cup whipping cream

1/4 cup sugar

1/4 cup Crème de Cocoa liqueur

1 teaspoon vanilla

1/3 cup coconut, toasted and crumbled

1/3 cup almonds, toasted and finely chopped

6 maraschino cherries, split (garnish)

Beat egg whites with cream of tartar and salt until they begin to stiffen. Add 3 tablespoons sugar and continue to beat until very stiff and satiny but not dry.

Whip cream. When it begins to stiffen add 2 tablespoons sugar, vanilla and liqueur and finish whipping. Fold beaten whites into the whipped cream mixture. Fold in coconut and almonds. Pour into 12 cups and top with 1/2 cherry. Freeze and serve.

Serves 12

COCOANUT PUDDING

Heat one quart of milk, then add three tablespoonfuls of sugar and one half cup grated or shredded cocoanut, one teaspoonful butter. Then add four tablespoonfuls Florida arrowroot starch, previously mixed with a little cold milk, then stir constantly until well thickened and creamy.

ARROWROOT DROP CAKES

Cream one-half cup of sugar with one-half cup of butter, beat separately three eggs, stir beaten yolks into butter and sugar, also a level cup of Florida arrowroot starch in which a teaspoonful of baking powder has been mixed; last add white of eggs little by little; flavor with grated rind of lemon, fill tins half full. Bake moderately to a light brown.

GUAVA PUDDING

Prepare guavas as for canning and stew until tender; sweeten to taste. Put in pudding dish or agate pan and cover with a batter of one cupful of flour, three quarters of sugar, one cupful of milk, one egg, one teaspoonful of baking powder, and one tablespoonful of melted butter, added last. Bake in moderate oven about half an hour.

CHOCOLATE COEUR A LA CRÈME WITH RASPBERRY SAUCE

2 ounces semisweet chocolate, coarsely chopped

1/2 pound cream cheese, room temperature

1-1/4 cups whipping cream

2/3 cup powdered sugar, sifted

1 teaspoon vanilla

Line 4 cup coeur à la crème mold with dampened cheesecloth, large enough to allow a 2-inch overhang.

Melt chocolate in a double boiler over hot but not simmering water. Cool.

Beat cream cheese with electric mixer until it is light and fluffy. Gradually add 1/4 cup cream and beat until smooth. Mix in sugar, vanilla and chocolate.

Whip remaining 1 cup cream to stiff peaks in another bowl. Gently fold into cream cheese mixture.

Spoon cheese mixture into mold. Fold cheese cloth over top. Place mold on rack in pan. Refrigerate 8 hours or overnight. Just before serving pull back cheese cloth and invert onto platter. Carefully remove cheese cloth.

RASPBERRY SAUCE

10 ounces frozen raspberries, thawed

2 tablespoons superfine sugar

1 tablespoon Kirsch

Purée raspberries and strain, pressing to get all the juice. Stir in superfine sugar and Kirsch. Pour over mold.

To serve, surround the mold with chocolate-dipped or sugar-dipped strawberries. Put raspberry sauce in a pretty dish to pass at serving time.

Serves 6 to 8

VELVET CHOCOLATE MOUSSE

3 ounces semisweet chocolate

3 ounces bitter chocolate

6 large eggs, separated

1/4 cup Tia Maria, Kahlua or Crème de Cocoa, mixed with 1 tablespoon of water

1/2 cup sugar

1/4 teaspoon cream of tartar

3 cups (1-1/2 pints) heavy cream

2 tablespoons sugar

Melt chocolate and cool.

Beat egg yolks until thick and lemon colored. Slowly add melted chocolate, liqueur and water (add more water if the mixture is too thick).

Beat egg whites with cream of tartar until soft peaks begin to form. Gradually add 1/2 cup sugar while beating. Beat until very stiff.

Fold 1/4 of the egg white mixture into the yolk mixture. Add remaining egg white mixture to yolk mixture and fold gently until no white streaks remain.

Beat whipping cream with 2 tablespoons of sugar until stiff. Fold whipped cream into mousse.

Pour into serving bowl and chill.

Serves 8

FROZEN CHOCOLATE MOUSSE WITH CRUST
(Variation)

1 cup flour

1 cup light brown sugar

3/4 cup almonds, ground

1/2 cup (1 stick) butter, melted

Preheat oven to 300 degrees.

To make crust, mix ingredients well and spread on a cookie sheet. Bake, stirring frequently for 20 to 25 minutes, until crisp. Cool and chop in processor with steel knife until medium fine.

Spray a springform pan with Pam. Cover bottom generously with the above mixture. Pour chocolate mousse in and freeze. When frozen add remainder of crumbs to top of mousse and freeze again.

Serves 8

Early Coral Gables arcade near Alhambra Circle

MISS FLORA

Seldom out of sorts or angry, she ran her pioneer school with strength and spirit ... Flora McFarlane came to Cocoanut Grove in 1886 as a companion to Commodore Munroe's ailing mother. After Mrs. Munroe's death three years later, Miss Flora accepted a position as the first school teacher for the fledgling school district of Cocoanut Grove. She plunged into her job with enthusiasm. The little school building overlooking Biscayne Bay, in what is now the business district of Cocoanut Grove, became a center of activity. School was in session during the week with lunchtime tutoring offered to adults who wished to further their education. Sunday was reserved for church services held by itinerant preachers.

In her spare time she organized the Housekeeper's Club to bring the women of the community closer together. That was a very important contribution, because the few local women faced a hard life, unbelievable workloads and a great deal of loneliness. A woman in pioneer Miami was expected to be wife, mother, field hand, doctor, midwife, deck hand, seamstress, cook, laundress and anything else that was needed.

Miss Flora was the first single woman to purchase a homestead block, 160 acres, for $1.25 per acre. The Royal Palm Ice Company on U.S. 1 now stands on a portion of that land.

McFARLANE MANGO MOUSSE

1 tablespoon (1 package) unflavored gelatin

1/3 cup cold water

2 cups mango purée

1/2 cup sugar

2 tablespoons lime juice

1 cup heavy cream

Sprinkle the gelatin over the surface of 1/3 cup cold water. Soak until it has absorbed the moisture and is translucent, about 3 minutes. Stir it into the mango purée with the lime juice and sugar.

Whip the cream and fold into the slightly thickened mango mixture and blend well. Pour into a chilled mold or any serving dish. Chill until set.

Serves 6

Pine Needle Club of Coconut Grove presents arms

CAKES AND PIES

ULIA TUTTLE, "MOTHER OF MIAMI"

Julia Tuttle, a lively, well educated woman, lived the life of a proper society matron in her hometown of Cleveland, Ohio. However, she lost her husband and father about the same time and decided to forge a new life for herself in the sleepy wilderness town of Miami. Her father, Ephraim Sturtevant, had left her the land he had homesteaded on the banks of the Miami River. Julia arrived with her two grown children and soon increased her land holdings with an eye on the future. She began to dream of a thriving resort area with hotels and tourists.

She realized that the railroad had to come to town and she pursued that goal relentlessly. In 1893, Julia Tuttle wrote to Henry Flagler about bringing his new railroad down to Biscayne Bay. She offered him half of her 640 acres at the mouth of the Miami River. (Flagler, who at that time was planning to extend his Florida East Coast Railway from St. Augustine only as far as Palm Beach, was not interested.) When the disastrous freezes of 1894-95 devastated the citrus industry in northern and central Florida, he was ready to reconsider his railway plans. Julia sent him a branch of orange blossoms to prove that the Bay area had escaped the hard freeze. Flagler was ready to talk business.

By that time Julia had persuaded the Brickells to include half of their holdings and the deal was accepted. On April 15, 1896, the first train rolled in, connecting Miami to the rest of the country. It was the birth of a new city!

TUTTLE'S LEMON POUND CAKE

The family name was made famous by Julia Tuttle who encouraged Henry Flagler to extend his railroad to Miami.

1 package Duncan Hines Lemon Supreme cake mix

4 eggs

3/4 cup oil

1 box lemon-flavored gelatin, dissolved in 2/3 cup hot water

Preheat oven to 350 degrees.

Thoroughly butter tube or Bundt pan.

Mix all ingredients on medium speed for 2 minutes. Pour into pan. Bake for 1 hour. Cool at least 25 minutes before removing from pan.

GLAZE

Zest of 1 lemon, grated

2 cups powdered sugar

1/2 cup lemon juice

Combine glaze ingredients, stirring well.

Pour 1/3 of the glaze over hot cake in pan. After 15 minutes punch small holes in cake and pour 1/3 of glaze over and into holes in the cake. Cool 15 minutes more, remove from pan and place on a cake plate. Slowly pour the rest of glaze over cake.

Garnish with thin slices of lemon or lemon candy.

Serves 6 to 8

BLACK WALNUT CAKE WITH CREAM CHEESE FROSTING

1/2 cup (1 stick) butter, softened	1 teaspoon baking soda
1/2 cup shortening	2 cups all-purpose flour
2 cups sugar	
5 eggs at room temperature, separated	
1 cup buttermilk	
1 teaspoon vanilla	
1-1/2 cups black walnuts, chopped	
1 can (3 ounces) flaked coconut	
1/2 teaspoon cream of tartar	

Preheat oven to 350 degrees.

Thoroughly butter and flour three 9-inch cake pans.

Cream butter and shortening. Gradually add sugar, beating until fluffy and sugar is dissolved. Add egg yolks, beat well.

Combine soda and buttermilk. Stir until soda is dissolved. Alternately add flour and buttermilk mixture a little at a time beginning and ending with flour. Add vanilla, walnuts, and coconut and stir thoroughly.

Beat egg whites with cream of tartar until stiff peaks form, then fold into batter.

Pour batter into cake pans and bake for 30 minutes or until cakes test done. Cool in pans for 10 minutes; remove from pans to finish cooling.

Spread each layer with cream cheese frosting. Stack layers and frost whole cake. Sprinkle top with chopped walnuts.

CREAM CHEESE FROSTING

3/4 cup (1-1/2 sticks) butter, softened
11 ounces cream cheese, softened
6-3/4 cups powdered sugar, sifted
1-1/2 teaspoons vanilla

Blend butter and cream cheese, add sugar and vanilla beating until light and fluffy.

Serves 10 to 12

CHOCOLATE MOUSSE CAKE

3 packages ladyfingers

2 packages (12 ounces each) semisweet chocolate chips

1/2 cup rum

1 teaspoon vanilla

8 large eggs, separated

Whipped cream, strawberries, or shaved chocolate (garnish)

Line the sides only of a 9 or 10-inch springform pan with ladyfingers.

Melt chocolate and rum over low heat. Remove from heat; add vanilla and stir until smooth. Cool slightly.

Beat egg yolks in a large bowl at medium speed. Gradually add chocolate mixture, beating constantly until thick.

Beat egg whites until they peak. Gently mix a small amount of whites into the chocolate mixture, then fold in the rest of the whites.

Pour into pan lined with ladyfingers. Top with whipped cream and decorate with strawberries or shaved chocolate. Refrigerate at least 3 hours.

Serves 8 to 10

154

POPPY SEED CAKE SUPREME

1 package yellow cake mix

1 package (3-3/4 ounces) instant French vanilla pudding mix

4 eggs, room temperature

1 cup sour cream

1/2 cup butter-flavored oil

1/2 cup cream sherry

1/3 cup poppy seeds

Preheat oven to 350 degrees.

Butter 10-inch Bundt pan.

Blend ingredients in large mixing bowl. Beat at medium speed 5 minutes, scraping sides of bowl frequently. Pour into pan and bake for 1 hour. Cool in pan on rack 15 minutes. Turn out onto a cake plate; cool completely before cutting.

Serves 8 to 10

CALAMONDIN CAKE

1/2 cup pecans, chopped

1 package yellow cake mix

4 large eggs

1 package lemon-flavored gelatin

3/4 cup salad oil

1/3 cup milk

1 ounce Grand Marnier liqueur

1/2 cup Calamondin Purée

Preheat oven to 350 degrees.
 Grease a Bundt pan and sprinkle bottom with pecans.
 Combine remaining ingredients; add batter to pan. Bake for 45 minutes. Cool and remove from pan. Cover with glaze.

CALAMONDIN PURÉE

Ripe calamondins

Sugar

Halve calamondins and remove seeds. Chop coarsely. Measure fruit into large enamel pot and add an equal amount of sugar. Boil rapidly to soft jellying point, stirring constantly.
 Ladle into ice cube trays and freeze. Put frozen cubes into heavy zip lock bags.

GLAZE

1/4 cup (1/2 stick) butter

1/2 cup sugar, or to taste

1 ounce Grand Marnier liqueur

1/2 to 3/4 cup Calamondin Purée

Heat glaze ingredients to boiling. Pour or spoon over cooled cake so fruit chunks stay on top.

Serves 8 to 10

M ARTI'S CALAMONDIN STAND
"On Miami Beach in the '30s most of us neighborhood youngsters had great fun catching crabs in Indian Creek, biking, swimming, tree climbing and going to 'bout every movie the Sheridan Theater ever ran.
 "Our lemonade stand was really a calamondin stand. Eventually we ran out of calamondins from trees and headed for oranges from home refrigerators to guarantee our revenue. That met with enough disapproval from our parents to effectively run us out of business. But it was fun, and we did pretty well. You see, folks who could eat a whole calamondin without making a face . . . got their penny back!"
 – Martha Pancoast Grafton, great-granddaughter of John Collins, who built the first bridge linking Miami to Miami Beach.

Fashionable bathing ensembles, 1922

COCONUT GROVE CAKE WITH COCONUT FROSTING

1 package yellow cake mix

1 package (3-3/4 ounces) instant vanilla pudding mix

1-1/3 cups water

4 eggs

1/4 cup oil

2 cups flaked coconut

1 cup pecans or walnuts, chopped

Preheat oven to 350 degrees.
    Grease three 9-inch pans.
    Blend cake mix, pudding mix, water, eggs and oil. Beat at medium
speed 4 minutes. Stir in coconut and nuts. Bake for 35 minutes. Cool in
pans 15 minutes; remove and cool on rack.

COCONUT FROSTING

1/4 cup (1/2 stick) butter, melted

2 cups shredded coconut

1 package (8 ounces) cream cheese

2 teaspoons milk

3-1/2 cups powdered sugar

1/2 teaspoon vanilla

Brown coconut in 2 tablespoons butter, stirring constantly over low
heat. Spread on paper towels to cool.
    Blend 2 tablespoons butter with cream cheese. Add milk, beat in
sugar and vanilla. Stir in 1-3/4 cups browned coconut.
    Spread each layer with frosting. Stack layers and frost whole cake.
Sprinkle with remaining coconut.

Serves 8 to 12

ALAMO APPLE NUT CAKE

3-1/2 cups tart apples, peeled, thinly sliced	
1-1/2 cups oil	
1-1/2 cups sugar	
1/2 cup brown sugar	
3 eggs, room temperature	
3 cups all-purpose flour	
3 teaspoons cinnamon	1/2 teaspoon salt
1 teaspoon baking soda	1 cup pecans, coarsely chopped
1/2 teaspoon nutmeg	2 teaspoons vanilla

Preheat oven to 325 degrees.

Thoroughly butter and flour a 10-inch tube pan.

Place peeled apples in cool water to keep them from turning brown. Set aside.

Combine oil, sugar, and brown sugar. Add eggs, one at a time, beating well. Sift dry ingredients together and add to the mixture. Blend thoroughly. Fold in apples. They need not be drained, just lift out with your hands. Add nuts and vanilla.

Pour into prepared tube pan. Bake for 1-3/4 hours. Cool in pan for 20 minutes. Turn onto wire rack.

GLAZE

3 tablespoons butter
3 tablespoons white sugar
1/4 teaspoon vanilla
3 tablespoons brown sugar
3 tablespoons whipping cream (optional)

Combine ingredients in a heavy saucepan. Bring to a boil and cook 1 minute. Spoon over warm cake. This cake freezes well.

Serves 12 to 16

MIAMI'S UNDEFEATED ALAMO

The building affectionately known locally as "The Alamo," from its fancied resemblance to the fort in Texas, was designed by August Geiger in 1917 in the Beaux Arts-Mediterranean style. It was Miami's first official hospital.

Constructed far out in the pine woods, it began service during the influenza epidemic of 1918 and has remained in the center of Miami's medical world ever since.

The gigantic Jackson Memorial Hospital complex grew up around the little building, almost engulfing it. In 1978 a concerted effort by Miami preservationists saved the small structure from demolition and had it moved to another site on the hospital grounds. Now restored, it serves as a visitors' center and a visual reminder of Miami's medical beginnings.

HE RAMBLE

"The Ramble" is the major fund-raiser for Fairchild Tropical Garden in Coral Gables. For many years the Ramble resembled a large fair where plants, crafts, antiques, rummage and food were sold. A special feature was the Tea Garden, a shady area where weary shoppers and workers could relax, chat and enjoy tea sandwiches and other treats. One of the Tea Garden favorites was this carrot cake baked by Nell Jennings, the widow of Colonel Robert H. Montgomery, who donated the bayfront acreage and named it in honor of his friend, botanist and plant collector David Fairchild.

The garden, dedicated in 1938, offers a stunning variety of tropical vistas. There are splendid palms from around the world and an exceptional variety of tropical and subtropical plants. Included are thousands of rare specimens from Asia, the South Pacific, Central and South America, beautifully displayed and thriving in this unique environment.

NELL JENNINGS' CARROT CAKE

2 cups flour

2 teaspoons baking soda

1-1/2 teaspoons cinnamon

1/2 teaspoon nutmeg

1/2 teaspoon cloves

1 teaspoon salt

Sift above ingredients together and set aside.

1-1/2 cups salad oil

2 cups sugar

4 eggs

2 teaspoons vanilla

1 cup coconut, flaked

1 cup nuts, chopped

2-1/2 jars of junior baby food carrots

Preheat oven to 350 degrees.
    Thoroughly butter 9 X 13-inch pan.
    Beat oil and sugar together until thick. Add the eggs, one at a time. Then add vanilla, coconut, nuts and carrots. Add the sifted dry ingredients gradually. Bake in a 350 degree oven for 50 minutes or until done.

GLAZE

1 tablespoon milk

4 tablespoons (1/2 stick) butter

1 teaspoon vanilla

1-1/2 cups powdered sugar

Heat ingredients but do not boil. Pour over warm cake.

Serves 10 to 12

COLLINS AVENUE CHEESECAKE

4 cartons (8 ounces each) whipped cream cheese, room temperature

2 cups sour cream, room temperature

1/4 pound (1 stick) sweet butter, room temperature

5 eggs

2 tablespoons cornstarch

1-1/4 cups sugar

1-1/4 teaspoons vanilla

1 teaspoon lemon juice

Preheat oven to 375 degrees.

Butter a 10-inch springform pan.

Blend cream cheese, butter and sour cream together. Add the cornstarch, sugar, vanilla and lemon juice. With electric mixer on high, beat until well blended. Beat in 1 egg at a time. Continue beating until mixture is very smooth.

Pour mixture into pan. Place in a larger roasting pan filled with enough warm water to come halfway up side of cake pan.

Bake for 1 hour or until top is golden brown. Turn off oven. Let cake cool in oven with door open for 1 hour.

Remove cake pan from oven and let stand at room temperature for 2 hours. Place on rack over sink or pan as cake pan will weep.

Cover and refrigerate at least 6 hours before serving.

Serves 8 to 10

Outing to Miami Beach, 1905. (Romer Collection)

COLLINS' FOLLY

Collins Avenue, Collins Bridge, Collins Canal … they all pay tribute to John Collins, a visionary hard-working Quaker, who saw agricultural promise in the overgrown sandbar we now know as Miami Beach. He first invested in an unsuccessful coconut plantation, and by the time he was seventy owned a five-mile strip of land (which would today be everything between 14th and 67th Streets).

To improve access to his farm, which grew avocados, mangoes, corn, potatoes, peppers and tomatoes, he dug the Collins Canal from the head of Indian Creek to the Bay. Then he got the franchise to build "the longest wooden vehicular bridge in the world." In November 1912, money for the bridge ran out half way across the bay — one mile short of the Beach.

Enter Carl Fisher, a wealthy razzle-dazzle promoter who knew a sure thing when he saw one. Collins needed $50,000 and Fisher wanted oceanfront land. They made a deal, and the two-mile-long Collins Bridge opened in June 1913. Everyone in town with a car drove over the bridge, turned around and went back — there were no roads on the island. The unlikely partnership of Collins and Fisher, based upon mutual trust, lasted until Collins' death at age 91.

159

"Skirts were long in those days and we held them high when walking the trails for fear of getting grease stains from palmetto leaves that had brushed against wagon hubs.

"Our neighbor, Mrs. Frazier, had a unique way of making us comfortable. When we visited her she sent her son Otto, Jr. to walk over with us. He walked ahead swinging a croker sack from side to side to gather as many sand spurs as possible lest we gather them on our skirts or stockings."

– Annie Mayhue Fitzpatrick, who arrived in Homestead in 1907. She lived with her aunt in a house "so small they put out the table at night instead of the cat so they could lower the cots that they hung from the ceiling."

CASINO CHOCOLATE CHEESECAKE

18 chocolate wafers	2 teaspoons vanilla
1/4 cup (1/2 stick) butter, melted	2 cups sour cream
1/4 teaspoon cinnamon	
8 ounces semisweet chocolate	
3 packages (8 ounces each) cream cheese, room temperature	
1 cup sugar	
3 eggs, room temperature	
2 teaspoons cocoa	

Preheat oven to 350 degrees.

Crush wafers with a rolling pin or in a blender to make 1 cup of crumbs. Add butter and cinnamon. Press crumb mixture on bottom of 8-inch springform pan; attach sides. Chill.

Melt chocolate in a pan at low heat.

In a bowl, using electric mixer, beat cream cheese until fluffy and smooth. Thoroughly beat in sugar, then eggs, one at a time. Add melted chocolate, cocoa and vanilla. Blend in sour cream.

Pour mixture into pan. Bake 1 hour and 10 minutes. Cake will be runny, but will become firm as it cools to room temperature. Chill in refrigerator for at least 5 hours before serving.

TOPPING

1 package (3 ounces) cream cheese
1/2 cup heavy whipping cream
1/4 cup powdered sugar
1 tablespoon Kahlua, Amaretto or liqueur of your choice
Shaved chocolate (garnish)

In a small bowl, beat cream cheese with an electric mixer until soft. Gradually add whipping cream. Mix at high speed until stiffly whipped. Blend in powdered sugar and liqueur. Cover and chill until ready to use.

Spread on cake and sprinkle with shaved chocolate.

Serves 8 to 10

GOLD STAR TARTS

(Carambola Fruit Tarts)

This recipe is from *Tropical Fruit Recipes,* published by the Rare Fruit Council International.

CRUST

2 cups flour

1/2 cup sugar

3/4 cup butter

1 egg

1 teaspoon vanilla

Mix flour and sugar; cut in butter until mixture is crumbly. Add egg and vanilla, mix until pastry holds together.

Divide into 15 muffin cups or tart pans. Press pastry against the sides and bottoms of cups to form the crust.

FILLING

1 package (8 ounces) cream cheese

1/3 cup sugar

2 teaspoons flour

1 egg

1 tablespoon milk or cream

1 teaspoon vanilla

15 slices of carambola about 1/2 inch thick, seeds removed.

Preheat oven to 425 degrees.

Soften cream cheese; stir in sugar and flour. Beat until fluffy. Add egg, milk or cream and vanilla; beat well. Pour filling into cups. Gently press a carambola slice into the top of filling.

Bake for 6 minutes. Lower the heat to 250 degrees and bake for 8 minutes more.

Makes 15

Note: Appearance and taste is best if tarts are served warm but they may be served cold.

REDLAND STRAWBERRY TART

CRUST

1 cup flour	1 egg yolk
1 tablespoon sugar	1 tablespoon ice water
6 tablespoons butter	

Preheat oven to 375 degrees.

Combine flour and sugar, work butter in with fingertips. Add egg yolk and ice water. Continue working with fingers until dough holds together. Don't overwork. Pat into a flat round and chill until firm, about 30 minutes.

Roll between sheets of waxed paper to fit 9-inch springform pan. Press the crust against sides and bottom of pan with finger tips. Prick dough with fork. Bake for 15 minutes. Set aside to cool.

FILLING

1 package (3 ounces) cream cheese
1/3 cup sour cream
1-1/2 quarts strawberries, washed and hulled
1/2 cup sugar
2 tablespoons cornstarch
Red food coloring

Beat cream cheese with electric mixer until fluffy. Add sour cream and beat until smooth. Spread on bottom of pie shell and refrigerate while preparing strawberries.

Using only the best berries, fill pie shell, starting at outer edge, pressing top of berries into mixture. Make a circle with points of berries up.

Mash enough leftover berries to make 1 cup. Force through a sieve and add water to juice to make 1 cup. Mix sugar and cornstarch with 1/2 cup water; add to juice. Cook over medium heat until clear and thick. Boil 1 minute. Add red food coloring until mixture is deep red. Pour over the top of the strawberries. Chill 1 hour.

Serves 8

MOTHER'S KEY LIME CHIFFON PIE

PIE CRUST

3 cups all-purpose flour	1-1/4 cups shortening
1 teaspoon salt	1/2 cup ice water, approximately

Preheat oven 425 degrees.

Two deep-dish pie pans, 10-inches each

Sift flour and salt into a mixing bowl. Cut shortening into dry mixture until it resembles coarse meal. Gradually add enough ice water to make a moist dough that holds together. Wrap dough in plastic wrap and refrigerate at least 1 hour.

Divide dough in half and roll each half about 1/2 inch larger than a 10-inch pie pan. Gently press dough into pans, taking care not to stretch it. Pinch edge decoratively and prick bottom and sides with fork. Line with foil and pie weights. Bake for 12 to 15 minutes or until golden. Cool completely.

FILLING

2 envelopes unflavored gelatin
1-1/4 cups fresh lime juice
6 to 7 eggs, separated
2 to 3 cups sweetened condensed milk
Pinch of cream of tartar
Dash of salt
3 tablespoons sugar
Whipped cream, sweetened (garnish)

Mix gelatin in only 1/4 cup of lime juice and heat until gelatin melts.

Beat egg yolks slightly, add milk and 1 cup lime juice.

Beat egg whites and cream of tartar with salt, gradually adding sugar until whites form stiff but not dry peaks.

Fold 1 cup of egg whites into yolks. Gently fold yolks into remaining whites. Pour into cooked crusts. Refrigerate for 2 hours. Top with sweetened whipped cream.

Makes 2 pies

Promoting Florida citrus

163

"Presto," built in 1885 by Munroe

MIAMI MINCEMEAT

Sterilize pint-size canning jars in a large pot of boiling water for 30 minutes while the mincemeat cooks. Have ready a canning funnel, a large spoon and tongs for lifting jars and lids.

3 pounds beef chunks, boiled (save the broth)

1-1/2 pounds suet, chopped

12 cups apples, cored, quartered but not peeled

Rind of 1 orange

Rind of 1 lemon

4 cups apple cider

1 cup molasses

5 cups sugar

1/2 pound citron

3 cups seedless raisins

1 teaspoon salt

Juice of 2 oranges

Juice of 2 lemons

1 tablespoon each, cinnamon, cloves, allspice, nutmeg

3 cups beef broth

Grind cooked beef, suet, apples, citron, rind of orange and lemon in food grinder.

    In an 8-quart pot with a lid, cook ingredients for 1-1/2 hours. Bottle in sterilized jars and boil vigorously for 30 minutes.

Makes 10 to 12 pints

Note: This recipe makes wonderful pies and tarts or you may include it in your favorite cake or cookie recipes.

LEMON CITY LOQUAT PIE

The loquat, a native of China, grows in most tropical and sub-tropical areas. This small ornamental evergreen has broad leaves and fragrant flowers. The fruit is small, round and yellow-orange with large black seeds; the delicious flesh is slightly acid in flavor.

Crust for 9-inch pie
3 cups ripe loquats, washed and seeded
1/2 to 1 cup sugar
1 tablespoon lemon juice
1 tablespoon flour, sifted
Butter

Preheat oven to 375 degrees.

Fill a 9-inch pie crust with loquats. If they are very ripe, sprinkle with only 1/2 cup sugar. If they are less ripe, increase sugar to nearly 1 cup.

Sprinkle filling with lemon juice and flour. Dot with butter.

Cover with lattice top crust and bake about 45 minutes.

Serves 6

"The Spirit of Florida," 1928. (Romer Collection)

BILLY'S BIGHT

Lemon City never had fixed city limits, and there is little evidence today that it ever existed. Yet, along with Coconut Grove, it was one of Miami's most important pioneer settlements.

In 1874 Billy Mettair settled on the shores of a bight on the upper bay which became known as Billy's Bight. "Buffalo Bill" Mettair was a rugged and colorful frontiersman who served as deputy, sheriff and local blacksmith. Twenty years later Lemon City evolved from Billy's Bight and became the largest town in Dade County. The name probably came from a lemon grove on the first homestead. The focal point of the settlement was the bayfront with its docks and boats. (Today's location would be approximately N.E. 61st Street.)

When the railroad came in 1896, development gradually moved west to the railway depot and away from the bay.

Lemon City had no local government — only an inattentive county government — so a citizen's group was formed to make local improvements. Their first project was to improve Lemon Avenue from the railroad crossing to the bay by covering it with crushed rock. The ladies raised money from box suppers, oyster suppers and ice cream socials.

The Lemon City area was incorporated as part of Miami in 1925.

SOUR CREAM PEAR PIE

6 to 8 large pears, peeled, cored, thinly sliced

1 egg, slightly beaten

1-1/2 cups sour cream

1 cup sugar

1/2 teaspoon salt

2 teaspoons vanilla

1/4 cup flour

10-inch regular or deep dish pie crust, unbaked

Preheat oven to 450 degrees.

Mix sour cream, sugar, salt, vanilla and flour. Add to pears and toss until coated. Pour into pie crust. Bake 10 minutes. Reduce heat to 350 degrees and bake until the fruit is tender, 30 to 35 minutes.

TOPPING

1/3 cup brown sugar

1/3 cup white sugar

1/2 teaspoon salt

1/2 cup flour

1 cup nuts, chopped

6 tablespoons sweet butter, melted

Mix topping ingredients. When pie is done, sprinkle topping over fruit and bake 10 to 15 minutes at 350 degrees. If crust gets too brown, cover edges with foil.

Serves 8

Note: This pie may also be made with apples or a combination of pears and apples.

MOCHA WALNUT TORTE

1 package (16 ounces) brownie mix, cake type

2 eggs, room temperature

1/4 cup water

1/2 cup walnuts, coarsely chopped

Preheat oven to 350 degrees.

Butter two 9-inch layer cake pans.

Stir eggs and water into brownie mix, then add walnuts. Pour into cake pans. Bake for 40 minutes. Turn out on rack to cool.

MOCHA TOPPING

1 cup whipping cream

1/4 cup brown sugar, firmly packed

2 tablespoons instant coffee granules

Walnut halves (garnish)

Whip cream until it begins to thicken. Gradually add brown sugar and coffee. Continue whipping until spreadable. Spread each layer with frosting. Stack layers and frost whole cake. Dot with walnut halves. Chill overnight before serving.

Serves 10 to 12

KAMPONG MANGO CHUTNEY

The Kampong, a beautiful estate in Coconut Grove, was the home of botanist David Fairchild and his wife Marian. She was the daughter of Alexander Graham Bell, a frequent visitor. Kampong, a Malaysian word, means a cluster of native huts.

5 pounds firm, ripe mangoes, peeled and sliced

1 pound preserved ginger, chopped

1 pound raisins

1 large onion, chopped

2 tablespoons salt

1/2 cup lemon juice and lime juice mixed

1 tablespoon cayenne pepper

1/2 teaspoon nutmeg

1 quart cider vinegar

4 pounds brown sugar

Garlic juice, to taste

Mix all ingredients. Cook 30 to 40 minutes and pour into sterile jars.

Makes 3 to 5 quarts

DR. PETERS' MANGO CHUTNEY

This pioneer recipe was submitted by Dr. Thelma Peters, renowned South Florida author and historian.

1 pound (4 cups) mature, unripe mangoes, peeled, finely chopped

4 cups sugar

3 cups sultana raisins, chopped

1/4 cup almonds, chopped

1/4 cup garlic, chopped

1/4 cup dried ginger, ground

1/4 cup dried chilies, ground

2 cups malt vinegar

Pinch of salt

Mix all ingredients together. Boil 20 minutes, stirring constantly. Pack in sterile jars, process and seal.

Makes 5 to 6 pints

SURINAM CHERRY RELISH

This decorative shrub, native to Florida, has distinctive fluted or ribbed berries. It makes delicious relishes and preserves due to its sprightly tart flavor.

3 oranges

1 quart Surinam cherries, seeded, chopped

2 cups celery, chopped

2 cups walnuts, chopped

1 cup sugar

1 cup water

1/2 cup vinegar

1 teaspoon salt

Grate zest of 1 orange and reserve. Section oranges removing all membranes. Mix all ingredients including zest and boil for 2 minutes.

Put in sterilized jars and seal with paraffin.

Yields 4 to 5 pints

MANGO HALVES IN GINGER SYRUP

This tropical treat can be served as a side dish or as a dessert sauce over ice cream.

1 pound mango sections, peeled, cut into chunks

1/4 cup Key lime juice

2 cups granulated sugar

2 cups water

1/2-inch piece ginger root

Select firm fruit, just beginning to show color. Cover mango chunks with lime juice. Cook in sugar syrup until clear. Let stand until cool. Pack fruit into hot sterile jars.

Add a piece of ginger root to syrup; boil until syrup is thick. Pour boiling syrup over fruit. Seal jars. Process 20 minutes.

Makes 2 to 3 pints

HOLIDAY CRANBERRY RELISH

1 bag cranberries, fresh, chopped or ground

8 ounces walnuts, chopped

3 medium apples, peeled, cored and chopped

1 jar (8 ounces) orange marmalade

1/2 cup white sugar

Combine cranberries, walnuts and apples. Add sugar and marmalade. Make up to a week ahead.

Serves 20 to 30

• • • • • • • • • • • • • • • • • • •

MALTESE SAUCE

Serve this wonderful Florida-style sauce with fresh asparagus, broccoli or green beans.

1 cup Hollandaise sauce

3 tablespoons orange juice

1 teaspoon orange zest

Combine all ingredients.

PEPPERY-MINT SAUCE

2 ounces water

1 cup fresh mint leaves, chopped

1/2 cup onions, chopped

1-1/2 cups fresh ginger, chopped

2 green chilies

1/2 teaspoon salt

Juice of 1 lemon

1/4 teaspoon red pepper

1 tablespoon sugar

Place all ingredients in food processor. Blend until the consistency of paste.
Cook over low heat for 5 minutes. Refrigerate.

Yields about 1 cup

• • • • • • • • • • • • • • • • • • •

MOUSSELINE SAUCE

Brightens the flavor of vegetables, eggs or poached fish.

1 cup Hollandaise sauce

4 tablespoons whipped cream

1/4 teaspoon garlic powder

Combine all ingredients.

Yields 1 cup

Yields 1 cup

HOLLANDAISE SAUCE

2 tablespoons white wine vinegar

2 tablespoons water

1/4 teaspoon salt

4 egg yolks

1 cup (2 sticks) sweet butter, softened

White pepper, freshly ground (to taste)

Dash cayenne pepper

2 teaspoons lemon juice

Combine vinegar, water and salt in small saucepan and reduce to 1 tablespoon over high heat.

Remove pan from heat, cool slightly. Add 4 egg yolks and stir briskly with wire whisk until thickened. Return pan to low heat and whisk in softened butter. Continue to beat the sauce until creamy. Blend in lemon juice, white and cayenne pepper.

Yields 1-1/2 cups

Note: To reheat, place over hot water and whisk vigorously.

BORDELAISE SAUCE

2 tablespoons butter

1 shallot, chopped

1 onion slice

2 carrot slices

Sprig parsley

6 whole black peppercorns

1 whole clove

1/2 bay leaf

2 tablespoons flour

1 can (10-1/2 ounces) bouillon, undiluted

Salt and freshly ground pepper, to taste

1/4 cup dry red wine

1 tablespoon parsley, chopped

Sauté in butter, shallot, onion, carrot, parsley sprig, peppercorns, clove, and bay leaf until onion is golden and tender. Add flour. Cook over low heat, stirring until flour is lightly browned.

Stir in bouillon, simmer, stirring until thickened and smooth, about 10 minutes. Strain.

Add salt, pepper, red wine and parsley. Refrigerate. Before serving, reheat sauce, covered, in a double boiler.

Yields 1-1/4 cups

"JOE'S STONE CRAB"
In 1913, Joe and Jessie Weiss opened a lunch counter at Smith's Bathing Casino on Ocean Beach. (It wasn't called Miami Beach until 1915.) They later moved across the street and opened the only restaurant in town.

He was urged to start serving the stone crabs which were plentiful in Biscayne Bay – the rest is history. The restaurant has evolved into a local gourmet landmark, while its stone crabs have acquired world stardom. Joe's Stone Crab Restaurant, still operated by Joe and Jessie's family, is a direct link with early Miami Beach.

We're indebted to Joe for popularizing stone crabs, the king of the sea. The texture and flavor of the claw meat is unique. The crab has two claws, one to fight with, one to feed with. Fishermen remove only the larger claw since the crab can regenerate either claw and be caught again and again for future feasts.

Marjorie Stoneman Douglas notes: "I would not use stone crabs in bouillabaisse. They are too good. You eat them for themselves alone. They are, I do think, the best shellfish in the world.

"I remember Havana in the old days. They used to have great casseroles of paella, rice and chicken with stone crab claws all over the top for decoration. You'd eat the stone crab claws along with the paella, but they wouldn't be mixed up in it. I used to love Havana so."

"JOE'S STONE CRAB" MUSTARD SAUCE

3-1/2 teaspoons Colman's dry English mustard
1 cup mayonnaise
1 teaspoon A-1 sauce
2 teaspoons Lea & Perrin's Worcestershire sauce
1/8 teaspoon salt
1/8 cup light cream

Mix all ingredients except the cream. Gradually, beating constantly, add the cream. Continue to beat at slow speed until it thickens to the desired consistency.

Yields about 1 cup

FLORIDA "OLD SOUR"

Key limes vary in size from golf balls to pecans. The juice is more tart than juice from other, larger limes. The trees bear only two crops yearly. Rather than do without, the pioneers developed "Old Sour." They seldom cooked with it but added it at the table as a seasoning for seafood or meats.

1 cup Key lime juice (use only ripe, yellow limes)

1 to 1-1/2 teaspoons salt, or to taste

Combine salt and lime juice. Let sit for 15 minutes. Strain and pour into a clean bottle. Let stand from 2 to 4 weeks until fermented. Refrigerate. To make the "Old Sour" hot, add 1 or 2 dried peppers before capping jar or bottle.

Yields 1 cup

Note: It can also be made without fermenting. If stored in the refrigerator, it will last 9 months. Shake before using.

Recipes from Dade County's first newspaper, The Tropical Sun.

September 23, 1891
"Lime juice. Take any quantity of ripe limes, roll soft, cut and squeeze juice out well. Strain with sandfly netting and boil down half. Strain and bottle well. One teaspoon of juice and two of sugar in a glass of water makes a pleasant drink. If iron nails are put in it, it is a good tonic."

March 23, 1893
"Recipe for Lemonade. To one quart of water add juice of three lemons and the rind of one. Cut just the outside yellow of the rind into tiny pieces and add to it two ounces of powdered sugar then pour over this mixture the water which has been heated to 'tea point.' Let cool."

(Of course there was no ice available in 1893 except when brought in from Key West by boat.)

BUNDANT FRUIT
The 1950's marked a turning point in Florida cooking. People began to take pride in regional foods. Newcomers learned from old-timers to enjoy the fruits of their dooryards: fresh citrus, loquats, papayas, and finger bananas that made a feast for the entire neighborhood when a bunch ripened. Fresh coconut cakes and pies were prevalent.

A shelf of sparkling guava and sea-grape jellies was a mark of a summer well spent. The only way to avoid the peculiar stink of overripe guavas (if you had a tree in your yard) was to gather them and make jelly.

A child in South Florida ran no risk of vitamin A and C deficiencies. Surinam cherries went into little mouths like sodas do today. The super-abundance of vitamin C in Barbados cherries (acerola) was discovered about this time and home growers used the juice in fruit punch.

As food editor of the Miami Herald, I dug up stories of Floridians' cooking – Pauline Hemingway's former cook in Key West who did crawfish enchiladas "like Miss Pauline told me," and recipes for exotic chutneys and jellies made for Fairchild Tropical Garden.
– Jeanne Voltz
Food Editor, Miami Herald, 1953-1960

TART-SWEET GINGER MARINADE

Use this tangy marinade with meat or poultry for a wonderfully different and exciting dish.

1/2 cup lemon-lime carbonated beverage
2 tablespoons soy sauce
4 teaspoons brown sugar
2 teaspoons garlic salt
2 teaspoons fresh ginger, grated

Thoroughly mix all ingredients.

Yields 1/2 cup

FROZEN GUAVA JELLY MOUSSE

2 eggs

1 teaspoon salt

1 jar (8 ounces) guava jelly

1/2 cup salted pecans, finely chopped

1-2/3 cups evaporated milk, thoroughly chilled

Beat eggs. Add salt, jelly, lemon juice and pecans and beat until well blended.

Whip chilled milk until stiff. Quickly fold in guava mixture.

Immediately pour into cold freezing trays. Freeze at lowest temperature.

Yields 3 pints

Fresh produce by the bushel

G UAVA WINE
"Guava wine. Mash 12 quarts of guavas and add one gallon of water. Let stand overnight. Squeeze out the juice. To each gallon of juice add 3-1/2 pounds of white sugar. Put in an open jar or keg. Skim off as it works. When it stops or nearly stops working put in a keg. In about a month rack it off and bottle. Resembles good sherry with a nutty flavor."
– The Miami Metropolis, 1896

C OFFEE BLUES
Coffee was in short supply and very expensive for the pioneers of the South Florida coast. One substitute was derived from the plentiful sweet potatoes. They were cut into small pieces and baked until charred. The charred chunks were then ground in a coffee mill and brewed like regular coffee. Served piping hot, the drink certainly had the same look as coffee but the taste was said to be somewhat like Postum.
– The Pioneer Cook by Donald Walter Curl.

MACADAMIA NUT BUTTER

Delightful served over steamed green vegetables.

Macadamia nuts, shelled

Oil

Butter

Place shelled nuts in 250 degree oven until they begin to tan. Cool, chop and then place them into a little oil and store in a jar in the refrigerator.

To serve, lightly sauté 1 tablespoon chopped nuts in 2 tablespoons melted butter.

. . . .

HONEY BUTTER

This is delicious served with toast, pancakes, or waffles.

1/4 pound (1 stick) butter, softened

1/3 to 1/2 cup honey

Cream the butter and gradually add the honey, beating until smooth. Pack in a crock, jar, or individual butter dishes. Refrigerate until firm. Will keep in the refrigerator for a week or so. It can also be frozen.

SWEET BUTTER

Make this days ahead for a special dinner party. It's easy and such fun for your guests, they'll love it.

1 pint heavy cream

Let stand in the carton in a warm corner of your kitchen until sour, at least 48 hours.

Pour into a glass jar with a tight lid and shake for 20 minutes or more. As butter separates and becomes firm add 1 or 2 ice cubes and shake butter gently until it becomes a firm round ball. Pour off all liquid and refrigerate until serving time.

. . . .

BUTTERSCOTCH SUNDAE SAUCE

1/3 cup butter

1 cup light brown sugar, firmly packed

2 tablespoons light corn syrup

1/3 cup heavy cream

Melt butter in a heavy saucepan over low heat. Stir in brown sugar, corn syrup and cream. Cook to boiling point. Remove from heat and cool slightly.

Serve warm or cold over ice cream.

Yields about 1/2 cup

Yields 1 1/4 cups

FUDGE SAUCE

1/2 cup (1 stick) butter

2/3 cup evaporated milk

2 1/4 cups powdered sugar

6 ounces bitter chocolate

Mix butter and sugar in the top of a double boiler; add evaporated milk and chocolate, cook over hot water for 30 minutes. Do not stir while cooking. Remove from heat and beat.

This will keep indefinitely if refrigerated. Reheat in double boiler. If you wish to have a thinner sauce add cream, not water.

Serve over creamy vanilla ice cream in parfait glasses.

Yields 1 1/2 pints

PRESERVED LYCHEES

8 cups lychees, peeled and pitted

4 cups water

3 cups sugar

Dissolve sugar in water and boil 5 minutes. Add fruit, bring back to a boil and cook until fruit is hot.

Ladle fruit into hot, sterile jars, cover with hot syrup and seal.

Yields 7 to 8 cups

Note: Serve with ice cream or as relish.

. . . .

THE INFAMOUS VELVET HAMMER

4 scoops vanilla ice cream, slightly softened

1/4 cup Crème de Cacao

1/4 cup coffee liqueur

Just before serving, place ice cream and liqueurs in blender. Blend until smooth. Serve in 5 ounce wine glasses.

Serves 4

WARNING
LAW REQUIRES
FULL BATHING SUITS
POLICE DEPT.

Law-abiding bathing beauties, 1934. (Romer Collection)

BIBLIOGRAPHY

Anderson, Marie, narr. *Julia's Daughters: Women in Dade's History.* Miami, Florida: Herstory of Florida, Inc., 1980.

Barbour, Alan G. *Humphrey Bogart.* New York: Gallahad Books, 1973.

Beater, Jack. *Pirates and Buried Treasure.* St. Petersburg, Florida: Great Outdoors Publishing Co., 1959.

Brookfield, Charles M. and Griswold, Oliver. *They All Called it Tropical.* 9th Ed. 1985. Miami, Florida: Historical Association of Southern Florida, 1949.

Cerwinske, Laura. *Tropical Deco.* New York: Rizzoli International Publications, Inc., 1981.

Curl, Donald Walter. *The Pioneer Cook.* The Boca Raton Historical Society, 1975.

Davis, Norma A. Davis. *Trade Winds Cookery.* Richmond, Virginia: The Dietz Press, Inc., 1956.

Dean, Love. *Reef Lights.* Key West, Florida: The Historic Key West Preservation Board, 1982.

Downs, Dorothy. *Miccosukee Arts and Crafts.* Miami, Florida: Dade Graphics, 1982.

Douglas, Marjory Stoneman. *Florida: The Long Frontier.* New York, Evanston and London: Harper and Row, 1967.

Douglas, Marjory Stoneman. *The Everglades: River of Grass.* Miami, Florida: Banyan Books, 1978.

Fitzpatrick, Annie Mayhue. *Lest We Forget.* Homestead, Florida: Unpublished manuscript, n.d.

Gifford, John C. *On Preserving Tropical Florida.* Coral Gables, Florida: University of Miami Press, 1967.

Jackson, Josephine. *Sunshine Cookbook.* Miami, Florida: Burdines, 1930.

Kent, Gertrude M. *The Coconut Grove School in Pioneer Days 1887-1894.* Coral Gables, Fl: Parker Printing, 1972.

Munroe, Ralph Middleton and Gilpin, Vincent. *The Commodore's Story.* Miami, Florida: Historical Association of Southern Florida, 1966.

Muir, Helen. *Miami, U.S.A.* Coconut Grove, Florida: Hurricane House Publishers, Inc., 1953.

Norman, Walter H. *Nicknames and Conch Tales.* Tavernier, Florida: W.H. Norman, 1979.

Parks, Arva Moore. *"The Magic City" Miami.* Tulsa, Oklahoma: Continental Heritage Press, 1981.

Peters, Thelma. *Lemon City: Pioneering on Biscayne Bay 1850-1925.* Miami, Florida: Banyan Books, 1976.

Peters, Thelma. *Biscayne Country 1870-1926.* Miami, Florida: Banyan Books, 1981.

Peters, Thelma. *Miami, 1909.* Miami, Florida: Banyan Books, 1984.

Rawlings, Majorie Kinnan. *Cross Creek Cookery.* New York: Charles Scribner's Sons, 1942.

Redford, Polly. *Billion-Dollar Sandbar.* New York: E.P. Dutton and Company, Inc., 1970.

Richardson, Dr. Mabel W. *Rare and Exotic Fruit of Florida: Tropical Fruit Recipes.* Miami, Florida: Rare Fruit Council International, 1981.

Silver, Doris S. *Papa Fuch's Family – 1881-1981.* Miami, Florida: Privately printed, 1982.

Smiley, Nixon, Ed. *The Miami Herald Front Pages 1903-1983.* New York: Henry N. Abrams, Inc., 1983.

C

FROZEN GUAVA JELLY MOUSSE

2 eggs

1 teaspoon salt

1 jar (8 ounces) guava jelly

1/2 cup salted pecans, finely chopped

1-2/3 cups evaporated milk, thoroughly chilled

Beat eggs. Add salt, jelly, lemon juice and pecans and beat until well blended.

Whip chilled milk until stiff. Quickly fold in guava mixture.

Immediately pour into cold freezing trays. Freeze at lowest temperature.

Yields 3 pints

Fresh produce by the bushel

MACADAMIA NUT BUTTER

Delightful served over steamed green vegetables.

Macadamia nuts, shelled

Oil

Butter

Place shelled nuts in 250 degree oven until they begin to tan. Cool, chop and then place them into a little oil and store in a jar in the refrigerator.

To serve, lightly sauté 1 tablespoon chopped nuts in 2 tablespoons melted butter.

. . . .

HONEY BUTTER

This is delicious served with toast, pancakes, or waffles.

1/4 pound (1 stick) butter, softened

1/3 to 1/2 cup honey

Cream the butter and gradually add the honey, beating until smooth. Pack in a crock, jar, or individual butter dishes. Refrigerate until firm. Will keep in the refrigerator for a week or so. It can also be frozen.

SWEET BUTTER

Make this days ahead for a special dinner party. It's easy and such fun for your guests, they'll love it.

1 pint heavy cream

Let stand in the carton in a warm corner of your kitchen until sour, at least 48 hours.

Pour into a glass jar with a tight lid and shake for 20 minutes or more. As butter separates and becomes firm add 1 or 2 ice cubes and shake butter gently until it becomes a firm round ball. Pour off all liquid and refrigerate until serving time.

. . . .

BUTTERSCOTCH SUNDAE SAUCE

1/3 cup butter

1 cup light brown sugar, firmly packed

2 tablespoons light corn syrup

1/3 cup heavy cream

Melt butter in a heavy saucepan over low heat. Stir in brown sugar, corn syrup and cream. Cook to boiling point. Remove from heat and cool slightly.

Serve warm or cold over ice cream.

Yields about 1/2 cup

Yields 1 1/4 cups

FUDGE SAUCE

1/2 cup (1 stick) butter

2/3 cup evaporated milk

2 1/4 cups powdered sugar

6 ounces bitter chocolate

Mix butter and sugar in the top of a double boiler; add evaporated milk and chocolate, cook over hot water for 30 minutes. Do not stir while cooking. Remove from heat and beat.

This will keep indefinitely if refrigerated. Reheat in double boiler. If you wish to have a thinner sauce add cream, not water.

Serve over creamy vanilla ice cream in parfait glasses.

Yields 1 1/2 pints

PRESERVED LYCHEES

8 cups lychees, peeled and pitted

4 cups water

3 cups sugar

Dissolve sugar in water and boil 5 minutes. Add fruit, bring back to a boil and cook until fruit is hot.

Ladle fruit into hot, sterile jars, cover with hot syrup and seal.

Yields 7 to 8 cups

Note: Serve with ice cream or as relish.

. . . .

THE INFAMOUS VELVET HAMMER

4 scoops vanilla ice cream, slightly softened

1/4 cup Crème de Cacao

1/4 cup coffee liqueur

Just before serving, place ice cream and liqueurs in blender. Blend until smooth. Serve in 5 ounce wine glasses.

Serves 4

WARNING
LAW REQUIRES
FULL BATHING SUITS
POLICE DEPT.

Law-abiding bathing beauties, 1934. (Romer Collection)

BIBLIOGRAPHY

Anderson, Marie, narr. *Julia's Daughters: Women in Dade's History.* Miami, Florida: Herstory of Florida, Inc., 1980.

Barbour, Alan G. *Humphrey Bogart.* New York: Gallahad Books, 1973.

Beater, Jack. *Pirates and Buried Treasure.* St. Petersburg, Florida: Great Outdoors Publishing Co., 1959.

Brookfield, Charles M. and Griswold, Oliver. *They All Called it Tropical.* 9th Ed. 1985. Miami, Florida: Historical Association of Southern Florida, 1949.

Cerwinske, Laura. *Tropical Deco.* New York: Rizzoli International Publications, Inc., 1981.

Curl, Donald Walter. *The Pioneer Cook.* The Boca Raton Historical Society, 1975.

Davis, Norma A. Davis. *Trade Winds Cookery.* Richmond, Virginia: The Dietz Press, Inc., 1956.

Dean, Love. *Reef Lights.* Key West, Florida: The Historic Key West Preservation Board, 1982.

Downs, Dorothy. *Miccosukee Arts and Crafts.* Miami, Florida: Dade Graphics, 1982.

Douglas, Marjory Stoneman. *Florida: The Long Frontier.* New York, Evanston and London: Harper and Row, 1967.

Douglas, Marjory Stoneman. *The Everglades: River of Grass.* Miami, Florida: Banyan Books, 1978.

Fitzpatrick, Annie Mayhue. *Lest We Forget.* Homestead, Florida: Unpublished manuscript, n.d.

Gifford, John C. *On Preserving Tropical Florida.* Coral Gables, Florida: University of Miami Press, 1967.

Jackson, Josephine. *Sunshine Cookbook.* Miami, Florida: Burdines, 1930.

Kent, Gertrude M. *The Coconut Grove School in Pioneer Days 1887-1894.* Coral Gables, Fl: Parker Printing, 1972.

Munroe, Ralph Middleton and Gilpin, Vincent. *The Commodore's Story.* Miami, Florida: Historical Association of Southern Florida, 1966.

Muir, Helen. *Miami, U.S.A.* Coconut Grove, Florida: Hurricane House Publishers, Inc., 1953.

Norman, Walter H. *Nicknames and Conch Tales.* Tavernier, Florida: W.H. Norman, 1979.

Parks, Arva Moore. *"The Magic City" Miami.* Tulsa, Oklahoma: Continental Heritage Press, 1981.

Peters, Thelma. *Lemon City: Pioneering on Biscayne Bay 1850-1925.* Miami, Florida: Banyan Books, 1976.

Peters, Thelma. *Biscayne Country 1870-1926.* Miami, Florida: Banyan Books, 1981.

Peters, Thelma. *Miami, 1909.* Miami, Florida: Banyan Books, 1984.

Rawlings, Marjorie Kinnan. *Cross Creek Cookery.* New York: Charles Scribner's Sons, 1942.

Redford, Polly. *Billion-Dollar Sandbar.* New York: E.P. Dutton and Company, Inc., 1970.

Richardson, Dr. Mabel W. *Rare and Exotic Fruit of Florida: Tropical Fruit Recipes.* Miami, Florida: Rare Fruit Council International, 1981.

Silver, Doris S. *Papa Fuch's Family – 1881-1981.* Miami, Florida: Privately printed, 1982.

Smiley, Nixon, Ed. *The Miami Herald Front Pages 1903-1983.* New York: Henry N. Abrams, Inc., 1983.

RECIPES INDEX